Pine Whispers

Biography and Writings
of
Marguerite Gahagan

Marguerite Gahagan Nature Preserve

Gahagan Nature Preserve Inc.
Roscommon, Michigan

Pine Whispers

Biography and Writings of Marguerite Gahagan

Marguerite Gahagan Nature Preserve

Selections edited and text written by: Tom Dale, Mary Hutchins, Brian Hutchins, Roberta Werle, Tracy Bosworth, Jeremy Jones.
Illustrations: Brian Hutchins.

Gahagan Nature Preserve Inc.
PO Box 421
Roscommon, MI 48653
www.GahaganNature.org

ISBN 978-0-615-69891-5

Printed and bound in the United States of America

Pine Whispers was written by volunteers. Profits earned from sales of this book are used to operate Gahagan Nature Preserve and its environmental education programs.

Contents

Dedicated to the memory of
Marguerite Mary Gahagan
writer, conservationist and lover of nature.

A special thank you to these people and institutions that contributed material or resources for this book.

Paul Barber, Print Foreman (retired), *Roscommon Herald-News*
Gary Boushelle, Michigan Department of Natural Resources (retired)
Clarke Historical Library, Central Michigan University
Dave and Penny Dilts, Gahagan Estate Executors
Keith Gave, Washtenaw Community College
Kirtland Community College Library
Kirtland Community College Print Shop
Otsego County Library, Gaylord, Michigan
Roger Rasmussen, Michigan Department of Natural Resources (retired)
Roscommon Area District Library
Roscommon Area Historical Society
Glen Sheppard (deceased publisher), *The North Woods Call*
Ilene Taylor, Housekeeper & Caregiver

Marguerite Gahagan Nature Preserve thanks the people who founded the Preserve and served on its initial board.

Back Cover Photo: Marguerite Gahagan caring for an ill racoon in her Roscommon cabin. From her personal collection.

Introduction

Please, could you make up a book called
"Pine Whispers?"

Divide into four parts for the four
seasons starting with winter. I'm sure
every subscriber would buy at least one
book.

I would like more than one to give as
Christmas gifts — even if it took five
years it would be worth waiting for.

Very sincerely,
Mrs. G. R.
Lake Orion, Michigan.

Letter to the Editor, *The North Woods Call* - Nov 2, 1955

The North Woods Call was a weekly conservation newspaper founded, written and edited solely by Marguerite Mary Gahagan beginning in 1953. Her personal column, titled "Pine Whispers," appeared on page three each week. It was filled with bits and pieces about her daily life, tales of her bird and animal neighbors and some vivid word imagery describing the nature that surrounded her. Marguerite never did package her "Pine Whispers" in a book as the reader above desired, but we have here, albeit some 55 years after this request. We are members of the Marguerite Gahagan Nature Preserve and our goal is to share the absorbing life story and a sampling of the prolific writings of this accomplished woman.

Miss Gahagan led a remarkable life that began in the metropolises of Toledo and Detroit before she changed gears, moving to the rural, north-central lower peninsula of Michigan. "A Writer's Story" is biographical, trailing her through these cities during her career reporting for big daily papers and authoring syndicated, serial stories. It continues with her move north to start *The North Woods Call*.

"News from the North Woods" features excerpts of her "Pine Whispers" columns illustrating mid-20th century life in northern Michigan small towns; times of two-lane gravel highways, rudimentary telephone service, the first days of television, general stores and difficult winters. Several columns show the tribulations of running a one-woman newspaper. Others illustrate her love of nature and wildlife; her "Little People."

In "Poetry from the Pines" we share her creative descriptions of nature, which often graced her "Pine Whispers" columns and were an obvious joy. We must note that we have edited most of these selections. Marguerite wrote these in narrative style and we fashioned her word images into poetic verse. The form is ours; the words and beautiful ideas are pure Marguerite!

In her final days, Marguerite left the public her great love – the splendor of nature. Her gift became the core of the Marguerite Gahagan Nature Preserve; an environmental education center and a wonderful natural oasis located in Roscommon, Michigan. "The Preserve" tells how this sanctuary came about and what you'll find there now. Visiting today, one can imagine Marguerite, the intrepid lady editor tapping out stories on her old manual typewriter; getting out one more edition of *The North Woods Call*.

- Marguerite Gahagan Nature Preserve

Marguerite Gahagan:
A Writer's Story

The Great Cocktail Mystery of March 12, 1946 took place in the swank Book-Cadillac Hotel, downtown Detroit. At 6:30, pals of Marguerite Gahagan, the gal reporter, were to move into the ballroom for a banquet at which many nice things were to be said of the way she had won the Heywood Broun Special Award.[1] At 7:30, a number of movie exhibitors were to eat in the Italian Gardens, courtesy of Allied Theaters. The Gahagan guests arrived first, each with a $3.50 ticket in hand, and were pleasantly surprised to find an elegant cocktail layout in the parlor next to the ballroom. They munched, mingled, and gulped and then moved into the ballroom at 6:30 leaving the cocktail room as dry as the Sahara. Only then did flabbergasted Allied Theater execs discover that all their canapés and good cheer had gone down the wrong gullets!

Unattributed news clipping from Gahagan's personal collection

In the line of duty, every newspaper reporter covers a banquet honoring an extraordinary citizen for signal service to the community. But the tables were turned that night. Nearly 300 Detroiters came to honor an outstanding reporter. The grand ballroom filled – a testimonial the magnitude of which had never been paid a member of Detroit's working press. Attendees included representatives of city and county government, schools and colleges, bench and bar, the clergy, labor and management and executives from all three of Detroit's large daily newspapers. They came to pay tribute to a young reporter who discovered, exposed and worked relentlessly to right injustices in the aftermath of one of the darkest periods in Detroit's history. At the time, Marguerite Gahagan worked the Wayne County Recorder's Court beat for *The Detroit News*.[2]

In July of 1943, while America was deeply embroiled in wars in Europe and the Pacific to protect liberty and justice, riots broke out in Detroit over those same values. Many people, both African-American and white, had moved into the city from the south to fill the many job openings as Detroit geared up for wartime manufacturing. Prevailing prejudicial attitudes and a terrible lack of decent housing for incoming African-Americans fed a fundamental distrust between the races which soon broke into some of the most horrific race riots in our country's history. These riots resulted in the loss of lives and countless acts of violence before being brought under control by federal forces. The riots brought great disgrace and dishonor to Detroit. Most of the 37 people killed were African-American. Only three people were ever convicted of murder.[3]

Marguerite felt that two of the convicted men, one white and one African-American, were victims of unfair trials. Aldo Trani, a white 16-year-old, was accused of killing Moses Kiska, an African-American. In January of 1944, Trani was found guilty and sentenced to 5-1/2 to 25 years in Jackson Prison. Miss Gahagan noted and reported discrepancies in the testimony offered by the prosecution's main witnesses, four juveniles, all with police records.

In March, Aaron Fox, an 18-year-old African-American was convicted of the murder of an Italian doctor who was killed by brick-throwing rioters during an attempted house call in an African-American neighborhood. Fox was sentenced to 7-1/2 to 25 years in Jackson Prison. Gahagan suspected that the prosecution's main witnesses in his trial, all juveniles, had been "coached" by police officers involved in both of the cases. Marguerite knew that political pressure for convictions existed and she did not believe justice prevailed in either case.

Following the two trials, Miss Gahagan began investigating possible grounds for reopening both cases. She met with witnesses and then talked to prosecutors, attorneys and many civic groups; all of whom eventually gave her primary credit for forcing new trials. Though temporarily stymied when Trani was denied a new trial by the Michigan Supreme Court, she turned her efforts to the Fox case. Marguerite persuaded the assistant prosecutor in charge of Fox's case to take another look. He agreed to visit a witness, held for robbing and looting during the riots, in Ionia Prison. There, in the presence of the prosecutor, the witness denied his previous testimony, admitting that Fox was not at the scene of the murder. Because of a strong recommendation by the prosecutor, forced by Gahagan's persistence, Recorder's Court Judge Joseph Gillis ordered a new trial. During the new proceedings, an eyewitness stated he had told the police officer investigating the murder that Fox did not throw the brick which killed the victim. When Judge Gillis heard this, he excused the jury and ordered the police officer, the attorneys and press representatives into his chambers. He screamed at the officer, "This witness is here now in spite of you. This case has smelled to high heaven all the way through. I am glad now that I granted a new trial." It took only 15 minutes of deliberation for the jury to reach the unanimous "not guilty" verdict. Fox had already served two and a half years.

Aldo Trani, however, was still in prison and Marguerite Gahagan believed he, too, was innocent. She continued to interview witnesses in his case. Three admitted to giving false testimony. Fearful of police action, each refused to tell the true story in court. Later, two of the witnesses were drafted into military service. Now unafraid of police reprisal, they wrote her from the South Pacific saying they hadn't seen Trani at the crime scene but had testified falsely because they were young and afraid of the police. A third youth, influenced by their action, also admitted his earlier testimony had been prompted by the police officer. Their affidavits became the basis of a motion for a new trial. The court exonerated Trani.

Judge Gillis later remarked that he "believed that it was solely through the efforts of Miss Gahagan that a great injustice was corrected and all credit should be given to her." The judge also praised Marguerite at her banquet, saying, "The day I granted the motion for a new trial I did it more to get Miss Gahagan out of my hair than anything else. I admired and respected her. She was the last one you could hide anything from. I am humble and grateful for her intuition and her work, done with very little cooperation from any official source."[4]

Also at the banquet, her managing editor at *The Detroit News*, presented a check matching the first prize of the Heywood Broun award, $250, and remarked that, "She has the crusading spirit of the reporter. She always fights for what she believes in, and usually the thing she believes in is right." Edward Jeffries, mayor of Detroit, acclaimed her "A new champion in the city of champions; a champion in the field of human relations." The Rt. Rev. Msgr. Edward J. Hickey, Chancellor of the Archdiocese of Detroit, spoke for Cardinal Edward Mooney. "His Eminence sends me with a message," Msgr. Hickey said, "Your praiseworthy act has won for our city a good name and helped redeem the shame we deserve for our race riot."

In her own speech, Marguerite was modest: "Neither I nor any one person was singly responsible for the fact that two unknown, socially insignificant young men know that American justice exists today. This meeting is an expression that in the city of Detroit the truth exists." For Miss Gahagan the ultimate reward was seeing justice prevail.

Gahagan received letters of gratitude from Trani and Fox in support of the Broun award. Shown on the next page, the letters convey the despair and relief at their incarceration and subsequent release.

Other honors continued to come her way as a result of her work during this time. She was one of ten Detroiters awarded Honor Scrolls by the Detroit Association of Women's Clubs for making outstanding contributions toward racial amity.[5] The **Michigan Chronicle** recognized her as one of eight outstanding Michiganians of 1946.[6] The Newspaper Guild of Detroit saluted her with its *Page One* Award.[7] She received the Detroiter of Goodwill Award in 1947.[8] Later, in 1954, Governor G. Mennen Williams appointed her to the Judicial Council of Michigan.[9]

Governor G. Mennen Williams waits to greet Marguerite Gahagan, 1954. From her personal collection, unknown photographer.

*Dear Editor
I am one among
Millions; who from reading
Mrs. Margarite Gahagan
Culum in the Detroit News.*

Sept 4, 1946

Dear Editor

    I am one among millions, who from reading Mrs. Marguerite Gahagan culum in the Detroit News. Knows she is for fairnest to all man kind. Here I a lad of eighteen tried and frame for a crime I did not comit knowing from her experience around court, that I was an innocene boy. While I was away she wrote colums on how unjust I was did.

    She wrote what she saw and heard. A lady reporter who might have lost her job for helping an innonce colore boy. In a case where prejudice had taken his freedom

    The only regret there is not more reporters like her. She is one of the findest reporter in the world. Miss Marguerite Gahagan

Sincerely Yours
Aaron Fox

*is not more reporters like
her. She is one of the
findest reporter in the
world. Miss Margarite
Gahagan.
Sincerely Yours
Aaron Fox*

A letter written by Aaron Fox to the editor of The Detroit News following his release from prison was part of the case presented to the Heywood Broun Award selection committee. Roscommon Area Historical Society collection.

Gentlemen,

This letter is being written to express my thanks for everything Miss Gahagan has done for me. If it weren't for her I wouldn't be out writing this letter now.

I am one of seven children, and it is pretty hard for my Dad to support the family on his income.

I was taken in custody and put on trial for first degree murder. My Dad didn't have much money so he cashed all his war bonds and mortgaged the house to help get me out. It was a long and complicated trial and Miss Gahagan was in court every minute. My conviction aroused her interest in my case. She came to interview me in the county jail and believed my innocence. Since then I can never repay her for everything she has done for me.

While I was in prison she has spent countless hours interviewing people and witnesses, comforting my folks, and getting legal counsel to help me get out of prison. I will never forget how many inter racial meetings she has attended and all the interest she has taken in my case. She has acquired everything that ever helped me to get out and God knows what I would have done if it wasn't for her. I can only say that God bless her and I wish there were a lot more like her.

I am now able to help support my family and help out around home. We have a little four acre farm which my dad and I are really trying to fix, and if it wasn't for Miss Gahagan this would never had been possible.

All I can say gentlemen is that I wish there was some way to repay her and to express my grateful thanks for her kindness and all the attention she has given me.

Yours truly,
Aldo Trani

will you please excuse all my mistakes?

A transcript of Aldo Trani's letter to the Broun Award Committee expressed his thanks to Gahagan. His comments provide insight into both the toll on his family brought on by the wrongful incarceration and the extent of Gahagan's involvement and commitment to the case. Marguerite's role in this and the Fox case far exceeded her job as a reporter. Much of it was done as a citizen who had the power of the pen. Roscommon Area Historical Soc. collection.

A Writer's Start

Marguerite was born on June 22, 1907 in Toledo, Ohio to Joseph and Maud Gahagan. She had two younger brothers, John and James.[10] As a young girl she attended St. Ursula Academy, a private, all-female Catholic school in Toledo. Even then she was active in her community: at her high school graduation in 1925, she was recognized for raising funds for the school's new gymnasium.[11]

She attended the University of Detroit, graduating with a BA in Journalism in 1930. Marguerite's extended family may have influenced her choice of study. Three uncles on her father's side, Tom, Will and George, all wrote for or edited turf magazines and newspapers devoted to the world of horse racing.[12] An aunt, Nellie Gahagan Hayes, one of the first newspaper women in Detroit, wrote "graceful and intelligent music critiques.[13]" While at the U of D, Marguerite was active in theater and served as editor and feature writer for the *Varsity News*. She developed and wrote a column, "Stage Whispers," that foreshadowed her beloved feature column, "Pine Whispers" in *The North Woods Call* decades later.[14]

The *Toledo Morning Times* hired Marguerite immediately after graduation. One of her first assignments was quite daring: she posed as a gangster's moll and entered Toledo's home for "derelict women." While there, she obtained eyewitness materials for a series of articles under the by-line "Alias Mary Scott." She told the stories, some heart-breaking and some heart-warming, of the women, down on their luck, who resided there.[15] This crusading instinct remained with her throughout her newspaper career. Never satisfied with skimming the surface, Gahagan dug deep into each story.

The ink had barely dried on that undercover story, when *The Times* cast Marguerite to write in a much lighter vein as *Limerick Letty;* a circulation-boosting contest. Letty provided a near perfect limerick and challenged readers to provide the missing last line. In all, 64 daily limericks were printed with a whopping $2000 awarded in prizes. *The Times* promoted the contest and the newspaper using glamour photos of the beautiful, 24 year-old Irish lass in poses around the city.[16] The daily limerick related to the day's photograph.

Said Limerick Mary to our mayor
I think your city very fair,
   But find the lost lines
   To my rambling rhymes
(write your own last line here.)

Toledo's Mayor William T. Jackson poses with Marguerite "Limerick Letty" Gahagan as part of the Toledo Morning Times' daily contest. Photo from Gahagan's personal collection.

She soon left *The Toledo Morning Times* and joined the staff of **The Detroit Mirror**. That paper, however, ceased publication a year later, and Marguerite became unemployed. As a solution, she created her own job by promptly becoming a novelist. She penned *Polly Goes to Town* in 1932 at the age of 26 and signed a contract with the George Matthew Adams Service of New York. Her novel was syndicated to newspapers in 26 chapter installments. **The Detroit Times** hired her that same year. She continued her dual careers as fiction writer and news reporter for some time, completing five more novels in the next six years. These were syndicated in 672 newspapers in the United States and translated into Spanish for printing in 200 Latin American newspapers.[17]

Gahagan's Syndicated, Serial-Form Novels[18]

Polly Goes To Town, 1932. George Matthew Adams Service.

Love Happens Along, 1934. George Matthew Adams Service.

Love in the Ring, 1936? (Syndication firm unknown.)

Hit-Run Love, 1938. NEA Service, Inc.

This Could Be Your Story, 1940. NEA Service, Inc.

Murder In Paradise, 1941. NEA Service, Inc.

Marguerite moved to **The Detroit News** in 1934 and began her longest-running job with a big city paper, working there for the next twenty years. For the first eight years, she worked as a staff writer and feature editor. In the early 1940's, Marguerite worked to unionize *The News* staff.[19] The campaign was

Early in her writing career, Marguerite appeared in many promotional photographs such as this one for her novel, *This Could Be Your Story.*

One promotional flyer stated, "Miss Gahagan's terse, staccato style brings a great American drama to life."

She was approximately age 33 in photo.

Photo from Gahagan's personal collection.

ultimately unsuccessful, but likely contributed to Marguerite losing favor at the paper and being demoted to the court reporter position where she remained. Marguerite later opined, "I guess they thought a convent girl wouldn't last there very long. I stayed on that damned beat twelve years.[20]"

Even her many awards following the race riots did not result in a promotion. She continued to support fair labor practices throughout her time in the city, serving as president of the Detroit chapter of the Association of Catholic Trade Unionists from 1949 to 1952.[21] This progressive Catholic group worked to strengthen unions and to oppose communism (widely feared at the time) mainly through publishing a newspaper called the *Michigan Labor Leader* which eventually became *The Wage Earner*.

She belonged to other activist groups including Americans for Democratic Action, the Catholic Interracial Council and the Michigan Committee for Civil Rights.[22]

By 1953, Marguerite was ready to leave her job, the city, and life as she knew it to follow a new path. At the age of 46, she gave *The Detroit News* her notice and moved to the "middle of nowhere."

Marguerite Gahagan was a local celebrity in Detroit when she was a Detroit News feature writer. Here she exits a carriage for the world premeire of Mc-Fadden's Flats at Ye Olde Avenue Theatre in 1939. From Gahagan's personal collection, unknown photographer.

Marguerite Gahagan in a casual photograph during her 30's. From Gahagan's personal collection, unknown photographer.

Call of the North Woods

Passing cars catch the last of the melting
snow water and splash. Asphalt dries.
Square foot of yard is sodden brown. Small
patch of blue is soot smeared, car tires
whine and truck roars. A robin chirps from
an isolated tree. A pigeon wheels and a
flock follows, sailing over city hall,
courthouse, factory, home. Starlings
gurgle in spring warmth and strut and
pose.

I stared out over the city and on the
river, through glasses, saw ducks, and
thought of the north woods, woods so dear,
woods so free, and with unthinking haste
rushed, pressed the button, listened as
the elevator chugged its way upward, and
took it up, up. I climbed the dusty steps
to the roof and outside felt the faint
awakening of spring, there on the high
roof housing so many, and looked out over
the vast city at twilight, out over the
river where ducks rested on flight north.

The North Woods Call – April 1, 1959

Above, Marguerite reflects back on her time in Detroit and
her motivation to move north to the "middle of nowhere" –
actually Douglas Lake, just south of Johannesburg, Michigan.
A letter writer once questioned her about the location:

Where, oh where is Johannesburg? I've
heard of the one in South Africa, but
where in the hell is Johannesburg, Mich.?

Marguerite replied:

"On the 45th parallel, halfway between
the equator and the North Pole, a farming
community, in Otsego County: one tavern,

The North Woods Call – April 21, 1954

This was quite a change from the Motor City. She first visited this beautiful area with her mother, Maud, in the early 1940's, at the invitation of Detroit family friends who owned Deerfoot Lodge on Douglas Lake. Soon the Gahagan family purchased a cabin of their own, on the west shore of the lake and spent vacation time there every summer. Marguerite treasured her days "up north" and following her mother's death in 1953, she made the family log cabin her year-round home. It would also become home base for her new enterprise, a one-woman newspaper operation.[23]

With much care and planning, Gahagan founded a weekly, conservation-minded newspaper, titled *The North Woods Call* – the first such weekly in the country. She was not only reporter, but also editor, publisher, layout developer, advertising salesperson, copywriter, billing officer, subscription person, mail room clerk and all-purpose errand runner. Her brother, John, helped out for the first few months, but then Marguerite was on her own. It was up to her alone to put together a timely, informative, interesting paper and have it ready to go each Tuesday morning by 7 AM for the long, 55 mile drive from Douglas Lake to Roscommon. There, the Matheson brothers, co-owners of The ***Roscommon Herald-News***, set their own paper aside and devoted the day to printing Marguerite's paper. Volume One hit northern Michigan newsstands on November 11, 1953.[24]

And so The North Woods Call will try to serve as a link between the woods and down below. Each week it will attempt to cover local community highlights. And most of all it will emphasize the sports and recreation features that make this portion of northern Michigan unique in the state.

The Call frankly admits that it means to promote the north woods. The more people who come to know and love the woods, bring assets in the form of business, money to develop roads, new schools, improved land, added interests and support of state conservation programs.

The North Woods Call - November 11, 1953

What prompted Marguerite to begin her own newspaper? Perhaps she had the dream while editing her college newspaper. Maybe the idea first surfaced when *The Detroit Mirror* stopped publication and she worked independently as a successful serial novelist. Or maybe the dream developed during the 12 years she worked the "jail beat" as the Wayne County Recorder's Court reporter. In any case, shifting her mind-set from the problems of a big city courtroom to issues in rural northern Michigan and shifting from being one cog in a very big wheel to being the whole wheel was a profound experience. A year into her new life, Marguerite reminisced;

One folded the big white sheet of paper, and then one folded it again and cut it at the creases. There were eight white pages. One lettered in The North Woods Call on an otherwise untouched page one. It was the first page one and there wasn't a single subscriber and there wasn't a single advertiser, but The North Woods Call was on its way because miracles take place in the north country.

It was a year ago and today there are people who read the "little paper", who even take two-year subscriptions with great faith and apparent pleasure, and there are advertisers, making it possible to make the paper a reality.

There is the big solid press down in Roscommon where the Roscommon Herald-News steps aside Tuesdays so The North Woods Call, coming down from Johannesburg, can be run off, and there are the Mathesons, Darrel and Elwin ever able to untangle the problems, to forget their publishers' worries to listen to mine.

The North Woods Call - November 2, 1954

The first edition of *The Call*, as she came to refer to it, covered Crawford, Montmorency and Otsego counties. It focused on the villages of Gaylord, Johannesburg, Vienna Corners, Lewiston, Atlanta, Lovells, Grayling, Red Oak, Luzerne and Mio. Roscommon County wasn't on her agenda initially, but soon would be. In the log cabin "city room," looking down from his place above the fireplace was Elmer, a 10-point buck shot long ago by a great uncle of Marguerite's who hunted to provide game for lumber camps around Atlanta, Michigan. Elmer looked down over a cluttered newsroom and listened to the banging of typewriter keys as Marguerite worked on the paper she hoped would represent and promote northern Michigan.

Editing a weekly paper in the north woods and out of a log cabin on a lake changes one's editorial habits.

Doing it the primitive way makes the paper a closer thing than working with the streamline efficiency of down below.

John's hunting knife makes an excellent paper cutter when small sheets are needed for heads. It also sharpens pencils well.

A box of .22s does a competent job as a paper weight.

And one never needs a waste basket with the fireplace always waiting for more.

The fireplace eats up paper. All of the first edition's dupes that stood for hours of sheer, torturous writing went up in a couple of minutes. That was proof positive of the old saying that there is nothing deader than yesterday's edition.

The North Woods Call - February 18, 1954

In the early years, Marguerite confessed to having a great deal of difficulty filling up eight blank pages of copy. At first she didn't know the area very well and she wasn't an expert in the outdoor life. She had yet to meet the many personnel in the Department of Conservation who would later provide her with critical natural resource information. But Gahagan had several things going for her; experience as a nose-to-the-grindstone reporter able to interview newsworthy subjects and dig out stories, a lively curiosity, a desire to learn, a strong work ethic and healthy doses of grit, determination and confidence.

Another factor in her favor, were the friendships she had made while vacationing on Douglas Lake; a critical support system as she began her new business. Stewart and Dora Welch ran the Johannesburg Post Office out of their home and more than once, in the midst of a howling snow storm, Marguerite was invited to set up shop there and compose the newspaper. On her way to get the fifth issue to press, Gahagan's car struck a deer. Friends came to the rescue. A cup of coffee settled her down and the Welch's used their phone to arrange a ride for Marguerite on the milk truck to Grayling, where she met up with Elwin Matheson to finish the trip to Roscommon. Two other Welch's, Wilma and Edna, later came down from Johannesburg in their jeep to transport Marguerite back to her

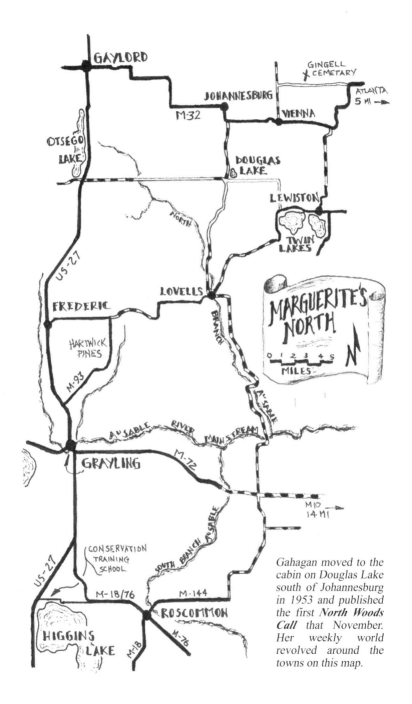

GAYLORD

GINGELL
CEMETARY

JOHANNESBURG

M-32

VIENNA

ATLANTA
5 MI →

OTSEGO
LAKE

DOUGLAS
LAKE

LEWISTON

NORTH

TWIN
LAKES

US-27

FREDERIC

LOVELLS

MARGUERITE'S
NORTH

0 1 2 3 4 5
MILES

HARTWICK
PINES

BRANCH

M-93

AU SABLE

AUSABLE   RIVER   MAINSTREAM

GRAYLING

M-72

M 10
14 MI

CONSERVATION
TRAINING
SCHOOL

SOUTH BRANCH AUSABLE

US-27

M-18/76

M-144

Gahagan moved to the
cabin on Douglas Lake
south of Johannesburg
in 1953 and published
the first **North Woods
Call** that November.
Her weekly world
revolved around the
towns on this map.

HIGGINS
LAKE

ROSCOMMON

M-18

M-76

cabin. That same winter, they took Marguerite deep into the swamp to help her find the perfect Christmas tree – the top of a bigger tree. And Dora and Wilma gave her a Christmas gift, an old cow bell that Grandfather Welch had made. Marguerite hung it on the porch and clanged it when she needed to warn her backyard birds of impending danger, such as a lurking northern shrike. Marguerite was grateful for her friends and told stories of their many good deeds in her paper.

There's snow in the air, despite promises of two weeks of good weather. And in the snow belt one takes precautions. The car is parked in the drive at the top of the hill to assure certain passage to the road.

Editions won't wait, and deadlines must be kept.

If the car isn't parked before the post office by 9:30 a.m. a rescue team comes out to the cabin to check. Wilma and Edna will jeep out, as they so often have before, to solve whatever major problem has upset the daily routine of living in the rugged north woods.

In this country one comes to know the true definition of "neighbor." It's different from the city definition. It literally means the dictionary definition: a fellow being subject to the obligations of humanity.

When one takes time to consider that definition, the beauty of it sinks in. And there is no better place to experience it than in the north woods.

The North Woods Call - February 18, 1954

Marguerite made new friends as well, and in fact, the entire town took an interest in her paper. News and feature tips written on scraps of paper and old envelopes, appeared in her car wherever it was parked. Locals would catch her up on what was happening in the area when they saw her. Merchants were proud when they sold out of her paper. People lucky enough to live in the middle of Michigan's hunting and fishing country seemed eager to share their good fortune with *The Call* and its readership.

Each town and township had its favorite gathering places and Marguerite knew and regularly visited them all to track down people and news. If an intended interview subject was not available, she left a self-addressed, stamped envelope with a list of questions. Marguerite did not have a phone at home; in fact, the nearest telephone was three miles away. This did not faze her, as most places in northern Michigan did not yet have telephones when she started *The Call*. Even as telephones became more common, she preferred her home and workplace to be quiet. There had been phones in the Detroit offices of *The News* and she had not liked the jangling interruptions. She put a lot of miles on her car as she made the rounds gathering news but it worked. She did not install a telephone until late in life.

The North Woods Call Evolves

From the beginning, *The Call* was dedicated to outdoor life in the north country and all those who enjoyed it. She filled the paper with articles of interest to hunters, fishermen, trappers, campers, canoeists, skiers and others who simply enjoyed the beauty of northern Michigan. Gahagan emphasized appreciation of nature and good conservation practices. She kept sportsmen abreast of changing laws and policies. Marguerite was concerned that the area she loved so much should be available to everyone and also remain intact for following generations.

> Would it be there in a hundred years for another to hear, to reach out and grasp, become a part of it, stillness alive, earth moving, starlight and firefly winking, capturing by being a part, to hold forever. Would it be there?

The North Woods Call – June 21, 1961

Early on, Marguerite discovered that every little town had old-time loggers, pioneers, farmers and merchants with amazing tales to tell. Each week she retold their stories, enchanting her readers and developing a remarkable treasure trove of area history. Many of her readers loved these recollections of days gone by. One old-timer told of reaching eighth grade at the age of 18 because he had worked three days a week driving a mail wagon and attended the one-room schoolhouse only twice a week. One year a lovely young teacher was hired and he became smitten with her. She felt the same way, and so the eighth-grader married his teacher! Others remembered days in the lumber camps. There was a story about a "cookie" using "sowbelly logs" for a solid week in the cookstove, when the rain made the wood too wet to burn. Though some stories were sorrowful, looking back on days when scarlet fever or diphtheria took too many lives, most were filled with a sweet nostalgia for the simple fun and freedom of days gone by.

Marguerite interviewed people, researched topics and scoured related media for information to educate and amuse her subscribers. Local happenings, such as who was catching brook trout and whose yard was visited by a pair of bluebirds, were included in a column called, "What's Happening Here and There." "Camp Talk in the Tall Timber" columns covered a variety of topics of wide interest. "Woods Gourmet" gave recipes and tips for preparing wild game and fish. "On the Bookshelf" promoted new books about outdoor sports and resource conservation, as well as books for children. "Wild Wings" brought readers news about birds. "In the Woods" presented facts about forests. "Finny Facts" featured fishing lore. "Michigan Quizdown" challenged readers to learn about the state. Starting in 1957, two new columns written by "stringers," appeared in *The Call.* Jerry Randall wrote "Man's Best Friend" about the raising and training of dogs. Lee Smits contributed "In the Open," a thoughtful column on conservation issues And, "Pine Whispers," "Out of the Mail Pouch" and Marguerite's editorials were must-reads.

Pine Whispers

"Your Pine Whispers brings out the sunshine on the gloomiest days..."

G.D.R., Lake Orion, MI
The North Woods Call - December 5, 1956

A favorite column for many was the one Marguerite called "Pine Whispers." This column was a mix of topics and styles. It was something of a free-wheeling, catch-all, composed partly of stories about Marguerite's life. Experiences from her week; funny, sad, frustrating or joyful – and her reactions – were shared and explored. She told of problems with winter driving, the challenges of meeting deadlines, which birds were visiting the feeder and of the satisfaction of rural living. She shared her views on current events and culture. The column became a running narrative of her life. Through "Pine Whispers," her readers came to know the woman behind the typewriter.

Marguerite also let her creative muse loose here, penning lovely, poetic descriptions of the outdoors throughout the four seasons. She noted changes great and small in weather and the flora and fauna. Readers raved about these selections and repeatedly asked her to reproduce them in a book. She invariably replied that she didn't have any connections in the publishing world.

> The Pine Whispers column you write is sheer poetry and I hope you plan to put all of them in book form for lovers of the north to enjoy at any time.
>
> K.K., Flint, MI
The North Woods Call - Apr 17, 1957

"Pine Whispers" also included stories of the birds and animals that frequented her cabin yard. Readers followed their antics with great delight. Marguerite was drawn to this wildlife and established regular and generous feedings or "tea times" for her "Little People." The seeds, nuts, peanut butter, and other treats were an expense that subscribers to *The Call* generously donated to – often tucking an extra dollar in with their subscription renewals. Marguerite mentioned these donations often in her writing to let her fans know that the "grocery money" was put to good use and much appreciated by her hungry little pals. She was faithful about the feedings and lamented when her hectic schedule caused her to be even a little late.

> The tea table has no lace tablecloth but it is popular.
>
> To it come the elite of the north woods, manners not too perfect, but probably in accord with the Emily Post of the woods folks.
>
> It is an old tree stump, low, leveled off, with hollows filled with sand to make it even and resemble a tea table, which it is rather than a long, silver-laden banquet table.

On it each evening at dusk I put the tidbits
that I know my neighbors will enjoy:
peanuts, lemon – flavored jawbreakers,
saltwater taffy, suet, crackers, a treat
for a gourmet – be he of the deep woods.

The North Woods Call – July 6, 1955

Regular visitors earned names and Marguerite recorded her frequent and often comical conversations with them. She counted them among her dearest friends. There was Mr. Hoover, the philosophical (and hungry) chipmunk who was always ready with a word of advice. Buster Chickadee and his pal Butch Chickadee, along with their mates, raised broods near the cabin and seemed to know a lot about life. Other visitors included a rabbit named Mr. Snowshoes; Mr. and Mrs. Hairy Woodpecker, the model parents; Mr. Prettycoat, the peanut-loving gopher; and over the years, a long line of raccoons beginning with Little Fellow.

Little Fellow, a foundling raccoon that appeared in a box on her porch one morning, was the first of several raccoons to capture her heart. Marguerite fell in love with him immediately and so did her readers. "He's the most wonderful, prettiest, intelligent, best behaved, determined baby in the north woods," she wrote.

The "Baby Book" became a regular feature in the "Pine Whispers" column as Marguerite lovingly raised her new "pet." He was as mischievous as he was adorable and made himself at home both inside and outside the cabin, amusing himself while the human he'd adopted worked away at her typewriter, occasionally demanding a tummy rub or some play time. If ignored for too long, he was apt to swing from the drapes, break lamps, chew on copy paper or climb on the editor's lap and hit the keys with little black paws. One day, to distract him while she worked, Marguerite poured some grape juice left behind by a visitor into his dish. He liked it so much that she refilled his dish three times before discovering that Little Fellow, who was now lying on the floor as he lapped up the grape drink, was actually drinking "Kosher Grape Wine!" She confided to her readers her fear that the Conservation Department might accuse her of contributing to the "delinquency of a minor." Sadly, in just one year, Little Fellow became sick with that "raccoon disease," and despite a trip to the veterinarian, he did not survive.

> In the box is a copy of the paper and it is open at Pine Whispers where Little Fellow's baby book and 'teen-age goings on have been recorded. And on his Pine Whispers Little Fellow sleeps the long sleep with a large portion of the editor's heart held in his small, now-still black paws.

The North Woods Call – May 11, 1955

Marguerite had a special fondness for raccoons and even acted as midwife while one gave birth on her living room couch! Another raccoon, Little Brother of the Bear, was so tame that he was eventually allowed to sleep in her bed; though she was a little dismayed that he didn't stay at the foot of the bed as she intended, but worked his way up to the comfort of her pillow. Conservation officers warned against taking in wild animals as pets but Marguerite argued that they chose her and there was nothing to be done about it.

Sometimes animals were injured and needed to be nursed back to health which Marguerite did with gentle tenderness for a great number. She might feed them special food or administer a bit of whiskey with an eye dropper. To keep a close eye on her patients, she'd bring them into the cabin. Once or twice, she even took an injured bird or animal to one of the local

Gahagan, with some "tea time" treats at Douglas Lake - September 1958.

medical doctors for aid. When Gus, a grosbeak with a broken wing, objected to having his cage cleaned, it clamped its bill down hard on her hand. She decided to seek help;

> I needed expert advice. And I got it. I met Roscommon's Dr. Charles Oppy on Main Street. Dr. Oppy, boasting the handsomest beaver cap in town, said it was very obvious that Gus was extremely nervous. He needed calming down. Massaging my sore hand adorned with a large red V, the shape of an Evening Grosbeak's tough bill, I agreed. He said he'd write out a prescription and I could pick it up at the drug store.

And that's what I did. Harold Grieve had
it ready for me with my guest Grosbeak's
name all neatly typed out and directions:
two drops in two teaspoons full of water.
Now I am prepared for the next cleaning
session. All I have to do is to wait for
Gus to drink two teaspoons full of doped
water.

If that doesn't calm him down I suppose I
can always drink the tranquilizer myself.
Just one more wrestling match with Gus and
I'll need to.

The North Woods Call – January 20, 1960

Her Little People had a special place in her heart and at the feeders around her cabin; not so the predators. She definitely respected the role of predators in the cycle of life, but they were not entitled to feast on her friends. When a shrike, hawk or cat was in the neighborhood, she would get out her .22 caliber rifle and fire into the air to scare them away. She knew what cowbirds were up to as well and did not want them laying eggs in the nests of songbirds that would unknowingly raise cowbird babies at the expense of their own, smaller offspring. When she heard their song, she would hurry out to chase them away. Mostly she just relied on noise to scare off predators but on one occasion, she'd had enough and tried to get rid of the cowbirds permanently. Fortunately for the cowbirds, she was not a great markswoman.

Out of Our Mail Pouch

Another popular part of the paper was "Out of Our Mail Pouch," where letters sent by subscribers were printed. These letters proved she was successful in her quest to share the outdoors of northern Michigan with her urban readers. City people often thanked her for bringing a bit of the woods to them each week. Her letters also demonstrated that Marguerite quickly gained a loyal following that often responded to her on a very personal level. Sometimes a reader took her to task, but more often they praised and admired her work. When times were good, her readers rejoiced along with her and when she had a problem, they commiserated and wrote notes of encouragement. When one of her "pets" died, readers mourned with her and mailed letters of sympathy. Most subscribers renewed even when rates went up and reassured her that the paper was worth twice the price. Many tucked in

---

Samples from "Out of Our Mail Pouch"

"I have never thrown a copy of The Call away. I always pass them on to someone to enjoy who likes the north as we do."

M.M., St. Charles, MI

* * * *

"Your paper is like a personal letter each week."

O.I., Applegate, MI

* * * *

"Your paper is perhaps the best edited, most brightly written publication of its kind I have ever seen. Obviously it is a labor of love by an unusual and talented person."

C.H.C., Conservation Director
National Wildlife Federation, Wash., D.C.

* * * *

"…the editor of the NWC strikes me as one who thinks,…the articles are clear, straightforward, dignified, readable, informative, varied and extremely competent….The NWC editor is a mighty rare bird and has a fine newspaper."

S.B., Exeter, New Hampshire

an extra dollar or two to help defray the costs of tea time for the little critters. As the paper grew, the letters that came in were not just from Michigan but from many states and even other countries. Word of mouth was one factor in the newspaper's growing popularity.

Conservation Concerns

In weekly editorials, she took stands on issues and argued for policies she thought would most benefit the people of the state. She made a case for a raise in state park fees to accommodate the development of more sites at a time when parks could not handle the number of people looking to use them. She wrote that private land owners needed to concede to society's greater need for the Sleeping Bear Dunes National Park. She praised or criticized the Conservation Department and local governments depending on what was going on at the time. She often related issues faced in other states and countries to what was happening in Michigan, looking for parallels that would enlighten her subscribers.

As her knowledge of the area grew, she included more and more news collected from the Department of Conservation field offices. Roscommon became an important town to Gahagan for something other than printing; it was home to the Michigan Department of Conservation's Region II Headquarters. This was the center of the agency's field operations for the northern Lower Peninsula. Nearby was its Conservation Training School on Higgins Lake, now known as the MacMullan Conference Center. Important department activities, classes and six meetings a year of the Conservation Commission took place at the school.

As *The Call* matured, natural resource conservation became an ever more important focus and Roscommon became even more important to its publisher. She became a regular weekly visitor at the department's region and field offices in Roscommon. From there she headed out to the Conservation School on Higgins Lake and perhaps to the Forest Fire Experiment Station south of Roscommon. She also visited other department offices in Mio, Atlanta, Lewiston, Johannesburg, Gaylord and Grayling. She soon became known as a reporter who was fair, honest and trustworthy. Information shared "off the record" stayed off the record. Considering the political drama that sometimes played out in the Conservation Department of the day, that was critical. She kept confidences and went to work doing the research that allowed her to tell the story without implicating a trusting source.

Gahagan worked hard. She was a tireless researcher and writer and also a quick study who always strove to expand her knowledge. Then, as now, there were always controversial topics in conservation and Marguerite did not shy away from them. She reported on what the Conservation Department was doing and wrote editorials about the department itself as well as the hot-button subjects of the day. Taking a stand on the issues of poaching, deer and elk herd management, the use of wire on property boundaries, the bounty program, fishing restrictions, lamprey eels, the importance of public-owned land and the use of DDT among others, earned her praise from some and vehement disagreement from others.

> How long ago it seems: that day whipping
> out stories for the first edition… How
> wonderful the hopes, the vision of a paper
> that could deal only with the pleasant:
> old-timers and their memories, the sights
> and sounds of the lovely woods, the happy

tales of hunters and nature lovers.
Unknown were the complications of a vast
Conservation Department. I didn't know one
existed. But within a month I learned. No
longer could one honestly limit coverage
to the wonders of the north woods. A
monstrous organization loomed too big to
ignore. One had to start working a beat.
Just like back in Detroit, just like
12 years straight covering Recorder's
Court criminal beat for *The News*, looking
for fast angles, digging, fighting for
facts, making enemies, and the fun of just
talking to the Little People became a side
issue.

The North Woods Call – Oct 31, 1962

Deer

The deer herd and hunting were of great interest to readers.
Marguerite ran stories of big bucks and who got them. But
then there was poaching. Marguerite hated poachers whom
she compared to bank robbers, stealing from their fellow man.
On this issue, she especially criticized prosecutors and justices
of the peace who didn't seem to take poaching seriously. When
penalties were assessed at all, they were like slaps on the wrist
and the poaching continued. So when word got out about an
undercover operation by four Michigan State Troopers who
broke up a poaching ring in Mio, she heaped generous praise.

Deer herd management was also a divisive issue. Heavy
winter snowfall and poor habitat resulted in large winter deer
kills by starvation or by packs of wild dogs. The Department
of Conservation's researched-based answer was to reduce the
herd by issuing doe, camp and farm permits. Popular opinion
ran counter to that plan and resulted in a political solution
to remove deer herd management from the Conservation
Department's game division and place it instead with the

Conservation Commission. The Michigan Legislature created eight regional citizen advisory committees that were to study, debate and survey public opinion and advise the Commission. Deer management was eventually returned to the Department, but not until after a long and heated debate. *The Call* recorded it all and editorialized for scientific deer herd management but with better education of the public on this issue.

> The (deer) opener, like it or not, was a long awaited vindication of the Conservation Department's Game Division management program. That three-day any-deer hunt at the end of the regular bucks-only season brought only public revolt and distrust that has carried on until today ... All that remains is educating the public "experts," a harder task than managing the white-tails.

An Opener That is a Vindication - Nov 27, 1963

Elk

Poaching was also a serious problem for Michigan's struggling elk herd. Michigan's native elk disappeared around 1875. Following several failures, five Wyoming elk were released in the Pigeon River Country in 1925 and grew to nearly 1500 by the mid 1960's. The herd reached the point where a limited hunting season was possible in 1964 and 1965. *The Call* kept tabs on the herd and reported on the "appalling" poaching problem. Hunting was subsequently discontinued as both habitat losses and the poaching problem reduced the herd to just a few hundred.

> The protected elk are a drawing card. That they may not be harvested is incidental as far as their worth to the State is concerned. As meat in a deep freeze they are far less valuable per pound than per

pound on the hoof posing for camera fans and eager sightseers for whom they provide endless hours of enjoyment.

Asthetic Values - December 4, 1957

Wired Property

Another problem was the use of wire to enclose property in the north country. No trespassing signs attached to fence posts and trees, were inadequate according to some landowners. They stretched wire around the parameter along with the signs. Wire thus stretched tended from time to time to cut across two-track roads, long used by hunters to access favorite hunting spots. Out would come the wire cutters and the controversy raged on. *The Call* covered the whole thing.

That unwelcome wire may drive home a needed warning. Guard the remaining land owned by Michigan if you hope to hunt another year.

Wire and State Land - Nov 6, 1957

The Bounty System

The bounty system that paid substantial sums to bounty hunters and trappers was an important issue to Marguerite. The State paid bounties for taking any of the State's major predator species: bobcat, fox, coyote, and wolf. In 1953, the total paid out was $275,000. Wildlife biologists disputed the need for a bounty and argued that it was a waste of money, but politics kept the bounty on wolves intact for seven more years. The bobcat bounty ended in the Lower Peninsula in 1955 but continued in the Upper Peninsula. Lee Smits, noted Michigan conservationist and former Conservation Commission member, joined *The Call* as a guest columnist, writing *In the Open,* in July 1957. From his earliest days as a conservation commentator, he argued against the bounty system and was given much credit by Marguerite for its eventual repeal. Miss Gahagan had called for the repeal beginning in 1955.

> That Michigan is still among the backwards states in paying bounty money is due entirely to the state Legislature where a handful of selfish, vote-seeking politicians yearly manage to bury bills that would revoke this antiquated statute.

Time To Bounty Some Legislators - Jun 5, 1963

Fishing

In the early 1960's Marguerite found herself in opposition with the fledgling but soon-to-be very powerful Trout Unlimited organization. The issue, as framed by Trout Unlimited, was for large stretches of the AuSable and Manistee Rivers to be subjected to fishing regulations termed "quality fishing waters," meaning artificial flies only, restricted creel limits and "keeper" sizes. The Conservation Department's fisheries division, relying on research results, advocated for fewer restrictions. When the Department's director disregarded the study results and ruled in favor of Trout Unlimited's position, Marguerite objected in several editorials. She felt that the special restrictions, which were not supported by evidence at the time, favored an elite few at the expense of the common man.

> But to push for more restrictions in the light of the (Fish Division's) research gives rise to a suspicion that fewer fishermen are wanted on some streams and that only a select fraternity would thus enjoy them.

What Is Quality - February 24, 1965

VOLUME FIVE — NUMBER FORTY - FOUR   SEPTEMBER 3, 1958   PRICE TEN CENTS

Wheelman In Knee Britches

It Was 60 Years Ago And Leon Crank Collected Some Stories

He poked among the weeds in back of his farmhouse east of Atlanta, having to take a second look because his eye sight isn't so good anymore, and he wanted just those certain weeds his grandmother Polly Wilkinson learned from the Indians in Canada a century ago. If he could find them he meant to steep some, brew them into a bit of tea that was mighty good if a man had a little gravel.

He thought that if he could find some of those other grasses and herbs he might get around to mixing up another batch of her green salve. Better than stuff you bought.

Leon Crank was 80 in April and he's slowed down a little with the years. In fact he started slowing down when he split his foot. Dropped an ax on it while making a road. Couldn't work until spring so he stayed with his father at Mio, at his dad's shoe shop at the bottom of the hill. "He had a little brick shop there, too," said Leon Crank.

But before he split his foot he watched the woods change, working in the camps, helping his father homestead in Tuscola County near Cass City.

* * * *

Wheelman!

He remembered leaving home, striking out on his own, wearing his knee pants on that 20 mile walk to Sand Beach and landing a job on a boat hauling lumber out of Alpena. The Captain's wife cooked, and his two girls washed and looked after the crew—the Captain, the mate and young Leon Crank.

"I ..."

a load and the Captain sold the lumber he gave his girls and me each $30. It wasn't pay either. It was a gift. Pay was $14 a month."

But the old ship was doomed. Came the midnight when he was wheelin' her between Sand Beach and Port Huron and she just broke up, just like that. "We was layin' out there. Didn't ...

ventures at sea. He headed ba... to Tuscola County and ende... at Fairview where h... brother Alf was upen... for some of th... around there by... by teaching...

Short Opener May Whittle Down H... | *That Fast ... Is ...*

Lamprey Problem

The sea lamprey, a parasite that kills fish, invaded the Great Lakes through the opening of shipping canals. The invasion peaked at around the time *The North Woods Call* began. Efforts at control started to show some results. Weirs and electrical barriers placed at the mouths of important breeding streams intercepted thousands of spawning adult lampreys. By 1958 more than 6,000 potential lampricide chemicals had been screened before the first effective treatment known as TFM,[25] was discovered. Application of the chemical in the headwaters of spawning streams helped to cut the lamprey population to something approaching manageable levels.

The lamprey problem continues to this day, but in Gahagan's time, it was a disaster and *The Call* covered it with great dedication and knowledge. However, she also came to believe a view not widely held at the time; that the lamprey was neither the sole reason, nor even the main reason, for the decline and eventual destruction of the Great Lakes fisheries. Unregulated commercial fishing had set the Great Lakes on that path long before.

> If the experts of Ontario, the Lake States and the U. S. Fish and Wildlife Service advocate the uncontrolled commercial fishing of lake trout while spending close to two million dollars to protect them from lamprey eels, it would appear that some of the new poisons should be used on them instead.
>
> **Just Asinine - Apr 29, 1959**

Pesticides and DDT

In 1961, Marguerite began following the Audubon Society's study of Michigan's bald eagle population decline. Since the very earliest days of *The North Woods Call*, bald eagle sightings were newsworthy. By the time Rachel Carson published **Silent Spring**, the 1962 treatise on the effects of DDT[26] on wildlife, *The Call* had already published ten articles related to the decline of eagles and the possible link to pesticides. In the years following *Silent Spring*, the eagle problem worsened and Marguerite strengthened her resolve, advocating for restricting the use of hard pesticides and for a complete ban on DDT.

Today, decades after the ban finally went into effect, the bald eagle population in Roscommon County alone exceeds that for the entire Lower Peninsula of 1963.

> Let no one forget that bees and the ants,
> the birds and fish and the worms in the
> ground are as essential to mankind's well-
> being as a chemical company that boasts
> of its weekly paycheck to its thousands
> of workers.

Let No One Go For The Soft Sell - Jan 9, 1963

AuSable River Pollution

During her years living in the cabin on Douglas Lake, when the weather and roads would permit it, Gahagan liked to head south from Douglas Lake on her weekly trips to Roscommon. The trips would take her across the north branch of the AuSable at Twin Bridges. Occasionally, she would stop and take in images of that wild and pristine river. Some of those enchanted images would eventually find their way into her "Pine Whispers" column.

This was in sharp contrast to the image she would convey 12 years later when Water Resource Commission studies showed the AuSable River below Roscommon and Grayling to be badly polluted. Sewage, even that treated at the towns' disposal plants, when added to that from the septic tanks stretching

44

mile after mile along the stream negatively affected the water quality. At Grayling, the mill pond impoundment warmed the water, at times, 10 degrees higher than desirable for trout. At Roscommon, researchers described the water above the waste-water treatment plant as "excellent" but below the outflow, the sewage created very turbid and discolored conditions. A moderately heavy slime growth existed and the sewage odor of the water was strong for more than a mile. The AuSable was a sick river. The studies also showed, however, that the river could heal itself. Miles below the treatment plants, water quality improved. The study recommended cutting nutrients in the stream and lowering the water temperature. *The Call* championed the cause and today, waste treatment plants are state of the art, the Grayling impoundment has been removed and the AuSable is protected by green-belt zoning.

> In 20 years they may still appear as a thin line on a map and be marked "river" or "creek," but their slowed water will no longer contain trout or watercress or be the playground for otter or heron, canoeist or fisherman, for water warmed, filled with strangling vegetation, polluted with the seepage from thousands of septic tanks draining down into it, must be written off as lost...
>
> The Death Of The Innocent Victims - Aug 24, 1966

Gahagan in the News

A year after moving to Douglas Lake and achieving a small measure of success with her upstart newspaper, Marguerite was featured in **Page One**, the 8th annual yearbook of the Newspaper Guild of Detroit in an article by her long time friend and *Detroit News* colleague Frances D'Hondt.[27] In 1954, a year after she began *The North Woods Call*, Women in Communications, Inc. lauded her as a *Headliner of the Year* for "courage and ingenuity" in starting the paper.[28] Stories about her appeared in state newspapers and a short article about the "woman publisher without a telephone" ran in newspapers across the nation. Locally, Marguerite was named "Hunter's King," when the Otsego Chamber of Commerce broke precedent by honoring a female, for Marguerite's contribution to sportsmen.[29] She was named an honorary member of the Outdoor Writers Association – an all-male group at the time.[30]

Notoriety for Marguerite and *The North Woods Call* started to snowball. Telephone service did not exist at Douglas Lake. An important call from Chicago came into the Post Office in Johannesburg in the middle of a Spring blizzard in 1955. It then took three days for *The Call* editor to return the call. The voice on the phone asked if she would be willing to come to Chicago on April 20th and appear on the **Welcome Travellers** TV Show. After a shock-caused pause, she replied; "I'll be there." The big question was how? There were deadlines to meet, stories to write, ads to sell, proofs to check, and Tuesday April 19th was printing day at the *Roscommon Herald-News*! The Herald's co-owners, Darrel and Elwin Matheson and printer Paul Barber, hatched a plan. The paper was readied for printing a day early and Marguerite was off to the Tri-City airport and on to Chicago. Friends took care of tea time responsibilities at the lake as well. As a result of her TV appearance, letters and new subscriptions flowed in. It was a very good week.

All the publicity was good for business, but Marguerite had an age-old feminine concern when she was in front of the cameras. Keeping up with fashion was not a priority in her everyday life in the north country, but she was anxious to look up to date and stylish when she herself was the focus of a story. She fretted in print:

> It's enough to make feminine nerves jumpy. Get out the spring hat. What spring hat? The one that was new three years ago. But it doesn't look right. Harper's and Vogue's hats, high style that is, look different. What's happened in three years? ...Get out the silk print… Yes the print is still wonderful but what about the hemline? What's happened to skirt lengths? In three years plenty has happened, but in the north woods one fights snow and mud and dust and back trails, and Sunday clothes give way to weekday clothes of slacks and boots — high ones to get through the back trails if the car — ever faithful — should bog down… Suddenly clothes have become important.
>
> **The North Woods Call – April 13, 1955**

There were other occasions when Marguerite and *The Call* found themselves in the news, but none more noteworthy than her first appearance on Mort Neff's **Michigan Outdoors** program in August 1955. It took her back to Detroit and to the studios of WWJ–TV. She had many fond memories of her nearly 20 years working for the newspapers in Detroit, so it was a really big day. It wasn't until early the next morning, heading back up north, that the wonder of being on Mr. Neff's hugely popular show hit home; an audience of one million people had learned about *The North Woods Call*! Letters and subscriptions poured in until *The Call* was swamped. Mort Neff continued to promote *The Call* and to quote from it and years later he had Marguerite back on the program.

Marguerite and *The Call* were also featured in *Time* magazine.[31] She recalled being photographed all around the cabin. She pretended to be typing and "click" and again, "click." Then out to the feeders and "click" and then again, "click." This went on half the day as the *Time's* journalist asked her an unending stream of questions. The article, along with a picture of Marguerite with a fawn, appeared in the August 24, 1959 issue. *The Call* received another big boost in circulation. She enjoyed the resulting attention and reading the story, She did not like being referred to as Maggie, as *Time* did seven times![32] She preferred to be called Marguerite or Miss Gahagan.

The Move

> The north woods shivered, moaned, bent under more snow and the winds drifted roads again. Schools were closed. No one went fishing. Everyone shoveled. And The North Woods Call crossed fingers – every one – and pushed for one more issue. It's been a winter of close calls, too close, and good stories gone uncovered because I couldn't get to them. It was a winter to make a great decision. That decision was to avoid risking a missed edition and to work for better coverage of news. It necessitates a move of home base and this week we move. Home base will be near Roscommon which will be the mailing address henceforth of The North Woods Call.
>
> **The North Woods Call - February 25, 1959**

Gahagan constantly worried about missing an edition. The winter of 1959 was a brutal one and roads often near impassable. Marguerite found this difficult. She made the rounds of small communities every week and then got on the road again to get the paper to Roscommon for printing and then to the Post Office for mailing. Marguerite decided to move from Douglas Lake and relocate the "city room" of the NWC to Roscommon. The move had two advantages. It put her close to the printer and nearer to the heart of her news beat; the Department of Conservation.

She temporarily rented the old Gallimore boarding house, in the middle of Roscommon, a block from the Department of Conservation and a couple more to the *Roscommon Herald-News* office. Her belongings remained in boxes on the floor as Marguerite set to work on the next issue in *The Call*'s new office.

When that week's paper was in the hands of the *Herald-News'* print foreman, Paul Barber, Marguerite set off to complete her move. Heavy snow at Douglas Lake meant that the long driveway into the cabin needed plowing so the moving van could get in. Once loaded, the van became hopelessly stuck. The snowplow returned to pull the van out to the road. Meanwhile, Marguerite strung "guilt food" like Christmas decorations on trees near her cabin by the lake. She said good-bye to her animal friends before following the moving van to her next adventure.

Gahagan did not wait long. That night the electric power at the rental house went out and the plumbing froze. Trying to move into a dark house at night proved nearly impossible. Then the good folks from the *Herald-News* showed up and quickly unloaded the van. The Matheson's provided the day's final blessing by inviting Marguerite to their luxurious redwood home with hot water, electricity, food and a good night's sleep.

The next day, she was back at it. The electricity came back on and Marguerite rolled up her sleeves. She had a house to clean, a newspaper to get out and needed to find a permanent home for *The North Woods Call*. While her news gathering, ad sales, and copywriting continued as before, she now spent any spare time driving around or tramping on snowshoes scouting for the ideal land on which to build a new cabin.

In March, a gift arrived along with a note from a reader in Ohio. "I am not a painter. I only do it for fun. But you have so often mentioned your Chickadees." And there they were in oil, real as life; Mrs. Butch Chickadee and Mrs. Nuthatch along with Marguerite's favored confidant, the wise chipmunk, Mr. Hoover. The gift brought her to tears, as she remembered the years at Douglas Lake and the bonds she had formed with her Little People. She was sure, she told her readers, that cousins of her Otsego birds would help her find just the right place for a new home.

Then one day, standing at the end of a two-track road south of Roscommon, she heard the drilling thunder of a pileated woodpecker building its nest. Marguerite chose this spot to build her "nest" as well. On May 4, 1959 she purchased ten acres from Forest Wyckoff.[33] The acreage had a swamp with a creek running through it, and plenty of cedar, balsam fir and spruce. Near her proposed building site, giant red and white pines stood majestically. She would listen to the wind blow through these trees as she worked on her "Pine Whispers" column in the coming years. Marguerite had found her "little bit of heaven."

And most days for the rest of that summer she would be there, filling feeders, planning her cabin and watching the work progress. It became the inspiration for many "Pine Whispers" columns in the weeks to come. With Marguerite's close supervision, the cabin was built. When the front steps were finished, she sat on them and chatted with her new woodland friends. Seeing the garage walls go up was particularly exciting. No more shoveling the car out each winter morning as at Douglas Lake – plus it would be big enough to hold a pile of wood for the fireplace. An outside, freeze-proof faucet provided an outdoor water supply for fire protection and a way to wash the car.

Early in September, following a horrible day on the road, which included her car breaking down and a bee sting, Marguerite couldn't imagine things getting worse, but of

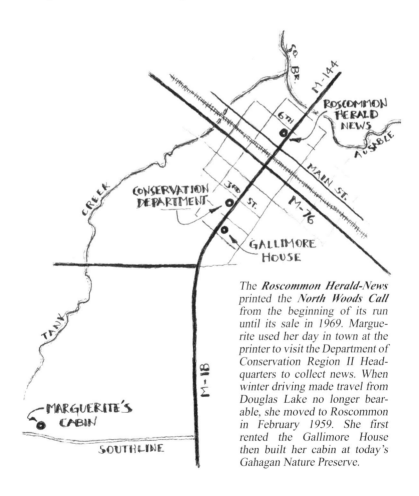

The *Roscommon Herald-News* printed the *North Woods Call* from the beginning of its run until its sale in 1969. Marguerite used her day in town at the printer to visit the Department of Conservation Region II Headquarters to collect news. When winter driving made travel from Douglas Lake no longer bearable, she moved to Roscommon in February 1959. She first rented the Gallimore House then built her cabin at today's Gahagan Nature Preserve.

*Marguerite looks over the printer's plates for an edition of the **The North Woods Call** at the **Roscommon Herald-News** in the mid-1950's. Photo from Paul Barber's collection.*

course they did. It was a very hot day and the printing press at the *Herald-News* quit working. *The Call* had to be in the mail by 4 pm. The efforts of Paul Barber and a dragged-in, beefed-up printing crew got the paper out the door – on time. The lady editor had had enough.

Needing a change of pace, Gahagan headed over to *The North Woods Call* acres to watch the construction. She had previously shown the builders a picture, written a memo and personally described her wishes for a fireplace designed to complement her Early American antique furniture. But the one she got was "ghastly," she wrote. The builders were chastised and a few days later, the unwanted brick fireplace was gone and in its place stood her new one with a beautiful wood surround.

In late September 1959, after seven months of living in town, Marguerite moved from her temporary lodging into her new home in the woods. And just like at the Douglas Lake cabin, the old cowbell was hung on the front porch. It was time again for "high tea." The tradition that began on the lake, resumed at her Roscommon cabin. *The Call* had a new address.

> Getting out the next edition will be torture. After all these months in town the windows will offer a much missed treat. How can a typewriter compete with the sight of my feathered neighbors, leaves turning before one's eyes, sunlight on gold brake, moonlight on pine branch?
>
> How good it will be once more to see the flames in the fireplace, hear the crackle of burning logs, smell wood smoke, and listen to the woodcock's cry. To see the sweep of sky and blazing stars, the streaming fingers of northern lights. To walk out the door on woods duff, drying leaf and brittle pine needle, the perfume of autumn all about one.
>
> The North Woods Call - Sep 23, 1959

And the paper kept growing. There were more awards and recognition. Over the years, *The Call* became one the most highly sought sources of news and opinions concerning the north woods and waters. The paper provided critical information to bird watchers, sportsmen, environmentalists and politicians. It was quoted in national conservation periodicals and won high honors from national and statewide organizations devoted to conservation of natural resources. In January 1966, the Michigan Chapter of the Soil Conservation Society of America presented Marguerite the Soil Conservation Certificate of Merit for outstanding service in furthering the cause of soil and water conservation.[34] In 1967, the National Wildlife Federation recognized her for outstanding conservation communication.[35]

Selling The Call

> One of the sad rights of being editor and publisher is that all mistakes are yours and yours alone. Nobody to blame. Just you. So don't ever envy an editor and publisher who is also chief cook and bottle washer and janitor to boot.
>
> The North Woods Call – Aug 14, 1957

The paper grew and Marguerite confessed that she was the "worst person" she had ever worked for. When she worked, and that was most of the time, she preferred not to be disturbed. She didn't have a telephone and she did not encourage visitors to her cabin. She wasn't antisocial but her work was her life and it left very little time for anything else. Marguerite often put in 12-hour or longer days, seven days a week, in seclusion at her cabin or on the road, covering her "beat." She traveled countless miles by car in all seasons and in all weather to gather news and deliver newspapers. She didn't take vacation days. If she was sick, or if the power went out, or the roof leaked, she still got the paper out. If one of her Little People required her company or care, even at inconvenient times, she was there for them but still got the paper out. When there wasn't enough news to fill the paper, she found news somehow and got the paper out. When the revenue from ads ran thin, she got the paper out anyway. When things went awry, like a newspaper being dated incorrectly, or pages accidentally printed backwards, or a stack of newspapers left uncut, she dealt with it and still got the paper out. As a staff of one she built a thriving business from the ground up, nurtured it and watched its circulation increase from zero to nearly 10,000 copies per week over the span of sixteen years.

What made *The North Woods Call* so special? The answer is Marguerite Gahagan herself. Marguerite **was** *The North Woods Call*. She had a vision and carried it through with skill and determination. She infused the paper with her own wit, vigor and personality while striving to maintain principled balance and logic in her reporting. She chose her own path, working hard at a job she loved, while surrounded by the nature that motivated and inspired her writing and sustained her spirit.

"What will happen to the *NWC*?" In August 1968, Marguerite posed and answered that question. The paper was for sale. No one editor and sole owner could go on forever. There were rumors circulating when Marguerite announced in the February 27, 1969 issue that she had sold *The Call* – still it surprised most of her readers. Glen Sheppard of Charlevoix was the new editor and publisher. She told friends at the Department of Natural Resources Regional Office (now the DNR, formerly the Department of Conservation) that she just felt it was time to move on. At 61 years old, after printing some 800 issues, Marguerite was ready for a break. Just the thought of sleeping in was sounding pretty good to her.

> There would be a heartache in writing "goodbye". And so I do not write it. I write instead that a long-time wish has been realized: I will, week after week, be able to write of the wonders of the north country in Pine Whispers, but with more time to write in peace, not rushed, ever pushed by a deadline as more and more copy must be written, and with so much to say but that must go unwritten because of the stress of a whole paper to write.

I must count my blessings, and they are
many. The burden is lifted …

The North Woods Call – Feb 26, 1969

Following the sale, Marguerite intended to serve as *The Call*'s editor emeritus, writing editorials for the new publisher. She continued in that capacity for less than a year.[36] Marguerite continued to write her "Pine Whispers" column, however, which was published in the *Bay City Times* until 1982. She also remained active in the politics of resource conservation in northern Michigan. Natural gas development in the Pigeon River State Forest was an area of great concern to her. She continued to visit the DNR Region II office and area field offices of the DNR for many years to get information for her column. When the DNR built the new Forest History Center at Hartwick Pines State Park, the conference room was named in her honor.

After Marguerite retired from writing the column for the *Bay City Times*, she continued to live in her Roscommon log cabin enjoying the outdoors and her animal friends. A life-long Catholic, she attended church regularly until health problems made it difficult. In her late eighties she became a victim of dementia and had to leave her cabin for skilled care in a local nursing home. She died on January 4, 1997 at the age of 89. She was buried in Gingell Township Cemetery near the four corners of Vienna, just a short drive from Douglas Lake.

Marguerite touched the hearts and lives of many throughout her life. She helped liberate two young men from lives in prison. By working to organize labor, she tried to better the lives of workers. She led on many conservation issues that affected her State. Through all the changes, from city to woods, from employee to business owner – writing was the common thread. Her typewriter was the tool she used in all her accomplishments. Gahagan's writings are her legacy. The wild, natural world was her other love. Her home in the woods became a nature preserve and now is also a legacy that will keep on touching hearts and lives for years to come. Through the Gahagan Nature Preserve, Marguerite continues to share the north country she loved with others.

Marguerite Gahagan in her '80's

A Timeline of Marguerite Gahagan's Life

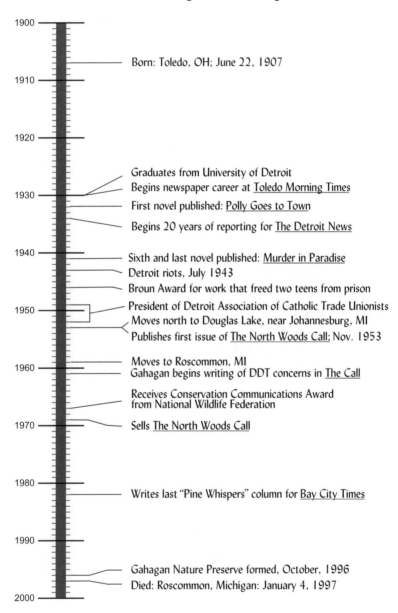

1900

Born: Toledo, OH; June 22, 1907

1910

1920

Graduates from University of Detroit
Begins newspaper career at Toledo Morning Times
1930
First novel published: Polly Goes to Town

Begins 20 years of reporting for The Detroit News

1940
Sixth and last novel published: Murder in Paradise
Detroit riots, July 1943
Broun Award for work that freed two teens from prison
1950
President of Detroit Association of Catholic Trade Unionists
Moves north to Douglas Lake, near Johannesburg, MI
Publishes first issue of The North Woods Call; Nov. 1953

1960
Moves to Roscommon, MI
Gahagan begins writing of DDT concerns in The Call

Receives Conservation Communications Award
from National Wildlife Federation

1970
Sells The North Woods Call

1980
Writes last "Pine Whispers" column for Bay City Times

1990

Gahagan Nature Preserve formed, October, 1996
Died: Roscommon, Michigan: January 4, 1997
2000

Reference Notes for Biography

[1] Heywood Broun was an outstanding newspaper reporter and editor of his time. He was one of the founders of the American Newspaper Guild in 1933 (now the Newspaper Guild). Each year the Guild presents a national award in his honor for outstanding reporting of a story. In 1946, the Guild felt that Gahagan's reporting deserved such an award but erred by not recognizing her. They created the Heywood Broun Special Award that year to correct this. She is the only one to receive one. (*The Detroit News*, October 25, 1946).

[2] Stoddard White, "Girl Reporter Sees Truth Made Real." *The Detroit News*. November 13, 1946.

[3] From the Heywood Broun nominating documents, 1946. The author is presumed to be *The Detroit News* staff. The document was found in Gahagan's personal collection.

[4] Stoddard White, "Girl Reporter Sees Truth Made Real." *The Detroit News*. November 13, 1946.

[5] *Detroit Tribune*. January 11, 1947.

[6] *Michigan Chronicle*. February 22, 1947.

[7] *The Detroit News*. February 6, 1947.

[8] Paul Gardner. *Pittsburg Courier* (Detroit). June 28, 1947

[9] *The North Woods Call*. July 14, 1954.

[10] Tom Dale, personal conversation with Ellen Gahagan, cousin. July 12, 2011.

[11] Unidentified Toledo, Ohio newspaper clipping from Gahagan's personal collection. May 4, 1925

[12] Don A. Lochbiler. "Hit-Run Love: Girl Reporter's Serial Starts Thursday." *The Detroit News*. September 11, 1938.

[13] *ibid*

[14] From Marguerite Gahagan's personal collection of news clippings. Date unknown. Appears to be from a University of Detroit publication.

[15] From Marguerite Gahagan's personal scrapbook of *Toledo Morning Times* memorabilia. Circa 1931-32.

[16] *ibid.*

[17] George W. Stark. "Scores Again: Miss Gahagan Writes Fifth Story." *The Detroit News*. September 8, 1940.

and Heywood Broun nominating documents, 1946. Gahagan's personal collection. Authorship is presumed to be *Detroit News* staff members.

[18] These syndicated novels, except *Love in the Ring,* can be found in various newspapers of the time or viewed on the internet using Google News and searching by her name or the title. *Love in the Ring* is listed in her Broun award biography but other information about this novel was not found. The publication date is speculative based on the roughly two-year spacing of her other serials. *Love Happens Along* was published in book form as well by Hillman-Curl, Inc. New York in 1939.

[19] *Wage Earner*. November 15, 1946.

[20] "Maggie of the North Woods." *Time*. August 24, 1959.

[21] Leslie Woodcock Tentler. *Seasons of Grace: A History of the Catholic Archdiocese of Detroit.* 1995

[22] "Newspaper Reporter to Talk Here Monday." from unknown Toledo newspaper. 1947 or 1948. This document was found in Gahagan's personal collection.

[23] France D'Hondt. "Where's That Gahagan?" *Page One: Newspaper Guild of Detroit Yearbook.* 1954.

[24] Tom Dale, personal conversation with Paul Barber, retired printer, Roscommon Herald-News July 13, 2011

[25] TFM is short for 3-trifluoromethyl-4-nitrophenol. According to the Great Lakes Fishery Commission, TFM kills sea lamprey larvae in streams with little or no impact on other fish and wildlife.

[26] DDT is short for dichlorodiphenyltrichloroethane. In 1939 it was discovered that this compound was an effective insecticide especially used to control malaria. It was banned in 1972 when evidence became clear enough, politically, that insects were not the only organisms harmed by the compound.

[27] France D'Hondt. "Where's That Gahagan?" *Page One: Newspaper Guild of Detroit Yearbook.* 1954.

[28] "A Brief History of the Detroit Professional Chapter, Women in Communications, Inc. *Women in Communications, Inc.* 1978.

[29] David L. Rogers. *The Bay City Times*. December 19, 1981.

[30] Marguerite Gahagan. *The North Woods Call.* November 2, 1955.

[31] "Maggie of the North Woods." *Time*. August 24, 1959.

[32] Letter from Dave Dilts, retired DNR Parks supervisor to Tom Dale. July 13, 2011

[33] County of Roscommon deed receipt. May 4, 1959.

[34] Award certificate in Gahagan Nature Preserve collection.

[35] Bill Stanczyk, Clarkston, Michigan donated Gahagan's trophy for this award to the Gahagan Nature Preserve. It had been sold at her estate sale and he discovered it at an antique store in Bay City, Michigan in 2012.

[36] Glen Sheppard published *The North Woods Call* for 42 years, until his death in January 2011. *The Call* was purchased by Mike Van Buren in late 2011 with intentions to relaunch the publication.

General Notes:

The personal collections of Marguerite Gahagan referenced above include newspaper clippings and news photos of her days working in Toledo and Detroit as a news reporter and feature writer. The Roscommon Area Historical Society has possession of these documents.

Gahagan's newspaper, *The North Woods Call* is the reference for most of the information about her life in northern Michigan. This personal history of Gahagan is largely autobiographical. The dates attached to quotes or articles from her newspaper provided much of the reference information and the text was derived from reading 16 years of her weekly publication.

News From the North Woods

During the 1950's and 60's, northern Michigan started feeling the reach of technology and modern improvements to which the city-dwellers (Marguerite referred to them as *down-belowers*) had become accustomed. Many of these new niceties appear to be things that she moved to get away from; the nuisance of telephones and televisions serve as examples. See what you think. We believe she moved to the north, in part, to escape modern life.

In *News from the North Woods*, we reprint selections of her "Pine Whispers" columns of life in Otsego, Crawford, Montmorency and Roscommon counties in the mid-20th century. These writings gave a clear picture of the trials and joys of a publisher and editor of a one-woman newspaper. You can feel the importance of the wildlife, the Little People in her life.

Our notes at the bottom of the columns give younger readers a perspective about the times and elaborate on issues found in the biography.

The Link

Under the tree is a toboggan trimmed in red.

It's polished wood will soon know snow, for it will be our link with the road and transportation.

On it will come the groceries, the papers; all the shopping. For carrying parcels or sacks, through the deep snow from the car, parked at the road, down the drive, down the hill to the cabin, can be a breath-shortening experience.

The toboggan is a gift from those who know what necessities are needed in a north woods winter. And so the gift is one to be grateful for, enjoyed and blessed as winter descends.

Dec 30, 1953

Life in a remote cabin of the mid-1900's had its "ups and downs." Toboggans served for more than fun. Like Marguerite, many parked their cars at the end of the drive and walked through the snow to their home in winter. Snow plowing was a luxury and when the writer moved north, her new neighbors gave her the perfect gift.

The Abandoned Ones

Ghosts of the old days, the days when the lumber camps boomed, the pine and hardwood crashed, and hearty pioneers moved in to start a new life in the north country, are bleak ghosts in the winter.

The cold, lonely ghosts are the old houses, the abandoned farms, the piled stones near the gnarled, the ancient apple trees back on the wood trails.

The woods have moved in closer, taking back the cleared land, the land cleared with back-breaking labor, and dried weedheads lift above the pile of stones hauled from the land that was to be farmed.

Wind-whipped houses, lonely, deserted, tilted by the wind, stand in clearings, lilac bushes pushing against sagging porches, the white snow's wind-pattern unmarked at the door closed upon nothing but memories.

Only the cold wind blows around the chimney, the stone chimney made by hand, stones dug, pulled, wrenched from the fields. The cold wind sings down the chimney to the cold fireplace before which once long ago the pioneers sat dreaming of the farm that would push the woods ever farther back and the wide fields of grain that would replace the pine and the hardwood.

Says an old-timer, gnarled as the apple trees he once set out, I built that house. Good hemlock, good cedar, good pine, good oak. Built it from the trees that stood there. Two floors it had, two floors because there was always wood. Built the window frames, fitted them in, walked to the town for the nails, built it all myself, my home, with my hands.

Feb 22, 1956

Lumbermen cleared the northern Michigan forests. Farmers followed, removing stumps, building homes and planting crops. The poor soils and short growing season of the region often led to failure, returning man's "improvements" to nature.

Evening Song

A story of the old lumbering days is recalled by Johannesburg's Tom Colbeck.

As he recalls it was back in the early lumbering days when he was a boy that he heard the story from an old timer who went hunting with a group of neighbors over around Spectacle Lake in southeastern Otsego County.

That night after the hunters had gone to bed, one thought he heard music. It wasn't the accustomed music of the wind through the trees, or the soft lapping of the lake water.

It sounded like the voice of a woman, soft and sweet with an instrumental accompaniment.

"I was afraid to mention it to the others because I figured they'd think I was a little balmy," the hunter explained. "But the next night I heard it again. Soft and sweet. So I woke some of them up, and they heard it, too.

"It was coming from across the lake. We decided to track it down. It just didn't sound real out there in those lonely woods."

The hunters found it was real enough. They came upon a covered wagon and a lean-to. And in the wagon was a piano, and a woman singing.

A family, coming from New York State, had stopped off at the lake. There were two children as well as the mother and father.

The couple had fallen in love despite parental disapproval. They had married, faced rough times, and started west with the children. And the piano had come along – a cherished bond with the life back east.

con't next pg

Evening Song

con't from previous page

Mr. Colbeck remembered the tale indicated. "They were really hard up. They had eaten roots, and any food they could find in the woods. But the woman still managed to smile, play the old familiar songs on her piano in the evening and sing for her husband and children.

"I often wonder what happened to them. No one around here ever knew. We never did get to hear the end of that story.

"But I'll always remember the story of that sweet music at night over on Spectacle Lake."

Nov 11, 1953

Marguerite needed stories, and lots of them, to fill her early editions. She interviewed "old-timers" in the Johannesburg area to dig up interesting tales. These pioneer stories helped build readership and are a treasure trove of Michigan history.

This sample is from the first edition of The North Woods Call.

Movie Night

It's summer in the burg.

Summer comes officially, for the folks who live in the area all the time not just weekends or summer months, when Tuesday night movies begin. School's out and farms are busy places with the young ones helping out during the dawn-to-dusk work days. The Tuesday movies are big social nights when farm families hit town, mingling later on with the summer people who flock up to lake and woods cabins.

Business places in the burg stay open, for it is the merchants who put the movies on. And mothers and fathers do the weekly shopping, going from store to car, arms laden with supplies for young and old who work the good earth. All round the school playground are rows of cars, farm trucks, pickups, '54 models chummy with vintage '40. And on the historic west brick wall of the old school is the screen which flashes the movie to the quiet audience.

Coming down M-32 one can hear the heroine pleading with the scoundrel lousing up her romance. Should this prove a bit thick for the very youthful portion of the audience they may trot across the road for an ice cream cone, or a handful of jawbreakers.

As have the young of countless generations of the past in countless small towns, young in the teen group sprawl on the grass; girls in little clusters looking not at the screen but at the boys sitting in their own little group and not as inattentive as they would appear to be.

The elders stay put, swatting visiting mosquitoes, hushing the very young, departing for a brief space of time into

Con't next pg

66

Movie Night

Con't from previous page

the make-believe world far removed from farm chores ever waiting.

Burg dogs, an important part of the resident citizenry, visit around. Sometimes folks visit other cars catching up on farm talk, township plans, the weather.

When movie night ends M-32 is a swarm of honking cars. Youngbloods do a bit of showing off taking the turn with tires squealing, horns blowing. Store doors bang as last minute customers make buys.

Quiet descends. Store lights dim out. Suddenly the little burg is deserted, still. Tuesday night is over. But for a few hours the lighted screen was the center of community social life in a small part of the north country.

Jun 9, 1954

A slice of life in Johannesburg during the 1950's. Rural northern Michigan was about to become more modern, but back then, it was still about locally owned stores and entertainment enjoyed with ones neighbors.

Antennas

The north country will never be the same. TV has moved in. Antennas sprout over log cabins and Von Horton put his up on a tree top out at Clear Lake.

Grooved juke box favorites are stilled as tavern and restaurant patrons watch bug-eyed at Cadillac's programs.

Polkas and tearful hillbilly favorites for '53 get a much-needed vacation. One wonders how long the unanimity of choice will continue among the patrons, all strong-willed individuals of set choice.

Jan 13, 1954

Television was established in Detroit before Marguerite's move, but not in the northeast Lower Peninsula. You needed a good, high antenna for even "snowy" reception from Cadillac – the closest source. Back in the early '50's, some smart tavern owners saw this as a way to attract customers and bought a TV set and antenna.

Marguerite never owned a TV and she lived until 1997.

What A Fate

What ever is going to happen to those Seagulls when the Straits ferry service is but a memory?

Their web feet have, with generations of mooching, developed fallen arches from walking on asphalt as they bum tasty tidbits from occupants of waiting cars lined up to take the ferry. They skim over the cars, hover with helicopter slowness, sizing up the suckers bug-eyed at the aerial display they put on, and then pick the one with the biggest sack full of crackers, potato chips, peanuts or stale sandwiches and move in en masse.

There are a couple of ancient veterans who have found out that by learning to catch a morsel in midair thrown from a car window they can cash in easily. Their less adept brethren scramble on the hot asphalt squawking and squealing and clashing wings, and finally collapsing again on the hot asphalt.

How wonderful it must feel when eventually they soak their callused web feet in that strange wet stuff; water.

Postcard hawkers have long missed a bet. They could have found a waiting audience ready to buy corn to feed the star actors at the straits, and has the union determined what is going to happen to those revered, honored, historic actors, the Seagulls, when cars dash across the bridge with not one stopping to watch a star perform?

Many people have been concerned about the future welfare of the ferry employees, but who has lifted a voice for the Seagulls whose antics have long entertained tourists and whose children and grandchildren will once again have to develop web feet for swimming instead of pavement hopping.

Feb 15, 1956

When the Mackinac Bridge began operating in November 1957, car-ferry service stopped, ending the long lines of autos and people waiting for the ferry. Marguerite speculated about one effect of the new bridge well before it opened.

So Beautiful, So Cold

Hauling in armloads of fire wood didn't raise the cabin's temperature or the editor's. Add another jacket, try to crawl into the open oven door, thaw out, and then remember there was still electricity, and so plug in the electric heating pad, and between chores hug the nice warm pad and thaw out.

Anyway the fireplace looked lovely. It sizzled, and cracked, and logs threw orange and red and blue sparks, and was beautiful and cold unless you crawled inside. But the stove, old faithful, steadily raised the temperature until if was 55 (if you stood five feet away) which was really warm, and after a thawing out I stood in front of it and pulled on long, cold red underwear and wool socks and two sweaters and managed to get dressed and drink a cup of coffee and head for Roscommon.

Feb 27, 1957

The Douglas Lake cabin was just that. Marguerite afforded herself little in the way of comfort.

City Room

The post office was open and the mail had arrived.

Armed with that, and the Welch typewriter, the city room was set up in their dining room until it was necessary to use that modern convenience, a telephone.

Then the city room moved to Ed's Village Inn, which it developed, was the hub of the universe that blizzardy day. Everyone wanted coffee, especially since the price hadn't gone up.

Everyone compared notes on his road, and who had to be hauled out, and who did the hauling.

The previous night's basketball game could be easily checked since the team's captain was there as final authority. Between Mae and captain Black, the team's percentage was worked out for the story.

Small town news on goings and comings added up to another few inches of copy for a paper that was stymied completely.

A typewriter appeared from under a counter and the city desk was set up in a booth while the clock hands traveled on and on, and nary a snow plow appeared.

Conversation got around to the dog poisonings and another story was ground out with considerable help from willing observers.

Someone else drifted in with an "item". Talk got around to the school's new girls' basketball team. Gradually the gaping holes in blank pages began to fill.

Mrs. Dreffs moved the city room into the big deserted dining room with the audience a bit removed.

Feb 2 1954

Snow at Douglas Lake made it difficult to get around her first winter. The Dreffs help out by donating space for The Call editor to work in town.

The Call

The phone call came during the blizzard and it was three long days before The North Woods Call editor managed to answer it. Chicago called, Chicago, the windy city, Sandburg's "hog butcher of the world," the city of the wheat pit, the Front Page, Hecht and MacArthur, port of the long boats.

The voice invited me to come and appear on TV. Back in the woods TV is something one reads about. In the little towns one questioned. What is Welcome Travellers?

They all knew the answer. "You are invited to be on that?" Awe-filled voices froze one with anticipation. How had TV, Chicago TV, heard of a little paper in the north country? It had and the voice said to come on and be our guest April 20 and something about presents. And one said, "gosh, I could use anything from a pencil sharpener to a typewriter" and the voice said "we'll put you up at the Sherman House" and one felt a sense of nostalgia for the city of Edna Ferber and "So Big" and the farmers' market and the Fourth Estate and said "I'll be there."

"I'll be there." How? How, with deadlines, stories, galleys to read, ads to get, proofs to check?

Tuesday, April 19 is printing day in Roscommon and the Herald-News is more excited than The North Woods Call. The Mathesons have it all figured out: the paper will be made up to the last period-except where The North Woods Call editor mismeasured copy and made up for a story two inches too long for the space-and ready to roll.

Make last minute changes, read last proof pages, grab a handful of papers and head south to Freeland and the Tri-City airport for a noon plane west.

Apr 13, 1955

Within a couple months of start-up, The Call's publisher gets some great news − a chance for publicity on a Chicago TV program. This led to similar invites and the subscriptions started to roll in.

Talk In The North

What are folks talking about these days in the north country? They're talking about telephones.

Even those natives who have never known anything but a well-jammed party line are talking about more phones, more lines, a better than one-in-a-dozen chance of getting the line.

To *down-belowers* trying to become natives, north country phones are as much of an experience as being snowed in. Business people grow red with rage, shake angry fists at the contrivance hanging on the wall, grind the handle with a vehemence indicating a wish that the "company" was inside the little box personally experiencing the grinding.

They look at the clock.

"Line's busy again. That would be Mrs. Smith; always starts visiting this time of the day," they say. They have endless stories about what Joe Doaks said to Mrs. Smith that time she wouldn't get off the line, and each community has a Mrs. Smith and a Joe Doaks. Now more telephones are coming to the north country. Civilization and progress march ahead.

"Won't you be happy when you can have a phone at **The North Woods Call**," they ask.

The answer is no – there won't be a phone. Still echoing in my ears are the live phones in the Recorder's Court press room in Detroit: five phones all ringing at once; ear-set clamped on one's aching head as stories were phoned in and the hands of the clock moved nearer another deadline.

A never-silent phone by one's bed ringing at all hours, late and early, a phone that one learns is not essential despite its convenience.

Feb 15, 1956

By the 1950's, metropolitan areas had telephone switches but in northern Michigan, operators still manually "plugged" through your call. Usually ten or so homes or businesses were wired on the same line. If your neighbor was on the line, you waited your turn – or listened in on your neighbor!

We Ask You

Well, bluntly, we don't want to fold up The North Woods Call. We are the only weekly in Michigan printing what you want to know. We are free, not bound by any club rules, not subsidized by even one gum drop, and we are a one-staff paper (that is if you don't count the prize reporters such as Mrs. Doe, Butch the Chickadee, Grandpa Hoover and the Woodpeckers).

But one has to eat. One has to buy gas for the long miles to drive to get the news, and there is that ever-growing mailing list.

It's been wonderful to look back at the honors such as Doe Queen of Otsego County in 1954, and Woman of the Year title bestowed by Michigan's Theta Sigma Phi at their Ladies of the Press party and to fly to Chicago to be on the national TV Welcome Travellers, and to really hit the big time on Mort Neff's famous show.

It's been heartening to read the stories spread across the U. S. by syndicates and to read the copy in such papers as The Toledo (O.) Blade written by Lou Klewer, past president of the outdoor Writers of America, and see reprints of North Woods Call stories in MUCC's Michigan-Out-Of-Doors and in Ontario's Conservation bulletins and praises in papers in Chicago and Indiana dailies.

It was nice to be on the Bay City radio August 31 on the Michigan Tourist Council Program, and, it's always nice to be liked and enjoyed and praised, but it takes hard cash to keep going. That's why we ask you to give us the benefit of your thinking: dare we raise subs to $4 a year?

The North Woods Call has always been the readers' paper. They seem to have charted its course and determined its content and with their letters made it reflect everybody's views. We'd like to keep it the way they want it. That's why we ask your advice now.

Sep 11, 1957

74

Four years into her North Woods Call endeavor, Marguerite muses about the finances of the paper, preparing her readers for a price increase. She could not live on awards alone! By the way, her readers – or at least those whose letters she later printed – gave her the green light to raise the cost.

What's Advertising?

Advertising didn't. We pounded the pavements of north woods communities. Yes, sir, everyone was willing to talk. They wanted to tell where the fishing was good and who caught what where and asked that you be sure to mention who stayed at so-and-so's resort, and when I said that was advertising and cost 70 cents an inch they headed the other way.

But I always went back to the towns because, since I'd first written on a blank sheet of paper The North Woods Call, certain ones had advertised and stuck by me, and you couldn't let them down and ignore their part of the north woods although 90 percent of the others were free riders taking advantage of somebody else's community advertising.

But the fact is there. Costs go up. It is there as one drives the miles to get the news, come home to write the ads, pound out the stories, make up the pages, gnash teeth over balanced heads, get groggy-eyed reading the proof pages, sweat out the deadlines, cry over their letters renewing subscriptions, bring their subscription cards up to date, weep over the bookkeeping so tough since one never had such training and two and two never makes four.

Sep 11, 1957

Frustration? You bet! Marguerite felt that she had a large hand in bringing hunters, fisherman and other tourists, with their money, to the North. In this "Pine Whisper" note, she vented about businesses that benefited from the exposure while her few advertisers paid the freight.

We Made It

Well, you got it. Last week's edition will never win a prize, but anyway it came out. Had we missed it, we would have lost our mailing permit and then would have come the, $64 question. *What now?*

And so another issue is out. I didn't dare risk that Tuesday deadline, our printing date. I headed for Roscommon Monday; that Monday that was 21 below. That Monday when no one's car moved, when it was a case of sweating it out, watching the clock, listening to the radio for weather reports ...

Feb 4, 1959

*The final straw? Marguerite endured six winters of driving from the Johannesburg area to Roscommon every week to get her paper to the **Roscommon Herald-News** for printing. Roads weren't as good — I-75 did not exist and some of the area's state highways were gravel — and the cars not as reliable as today. Marguerite soon moved to Roscommon to ease this problem.*

When reading her prose, it is easy to forget that she was the singular writer, publisher and editor of a weekly newspaper – any one of which could be a full-time job. Somehow she got it done.

Time's Effect

It was twilight and I sat where the cabin steps will come off the porch built for one purpose only: a place to feed friends when they come summer or winter. Mrs. Grosbeak came, gave a double take, but with great courtesy controlled herself. "My dear, you are haute mode," she said.

Yes, I was indeed high style. I had taken a 20-year leap. I had my hair style changed. There but a stone's throw from Robinson Creek I had not said a word of protest when Audrey said, "I'm going to do it different".

Now let me add a bit of background material for this terrific change. I had been subjected to Time. I, who had put so many old-timers through the mill, leading them step by step through life in the old north country, had been lead through the history of editor and North Woods Call by Time. I had also been shot, 60 times to be exact, looking at a pink moccasin flower, sitting on a pine log, looking over a lake, kissing a lady deer, typing copy for the next edition, standing in front of the Roscommon Railroad Station where copies depart for points east, west, north, south.

Jul 8, 1959

A writer and photographer from *Time* magazine came to Roscommon in July 1959 to write a story about Marguerite and *The North Woods Call.* It was a big deal; the publicity resulted in many more subscribers.

Marguerite wrote for the society page early in her newspaper career. She was high fashion for that job. Now six years in the north woods and she dressed down – yet probably not as much as we see people today. Her date with the magazine forced Marguerite to get a little style back and quickly.

Also note that the mail still came into and out of Roscommon by train in 1959. That would soon change.

Move

A new kitchen to get used to. And a new U.S. Mail Service to louse me up. Me and everyone else in the north country. Gone is the mail train. New is the truck, and everything was three days late last week. Even The North Woods Calls. The ones that should have arrived on Wednesday came on Thursday. Letters for the south went north.

All is confusion. Mail. Moving. And boxes. B u t the moment has arrived. The Call will be in its new home this week.

May 23, 1959

What a year 1959 was; February's move to a Roscommon rental, the search for a new home site, building a cabin and then a second move to the new home. In the middle of all this, the postal system changed how it moved mail in and out of town resulting in north woods chaos.

It Started

Then the snow started. The wind roared. Trees went wild. At 11:30 p.m. I stared outside. It was a pistol. And the next day was printing day. I set the alarm 45 minutes earlier than usual. It took me a half hour to wade through drifts to fill feeders while Grosbeaks talked spring-talk in the trees and watched me. I thought of how it would have been were I still living in the cabin just south of Johannesburg. I guessed I would have arrived at the printers in Roscommon about noon the next day. Life in the new cabin had been a breeze. So now late in March winter had arrived. I headed out my drive, road well protected by trees, and started gunning. I flipped on the windshield wipers. I braced. I was approaching the plains, that huge wide treeless stretch where the wind had free reign to build up drifts.

And I hit.

Prepared as I was for those drifts I couldn't control a reflex. When the car was engulfed in a sea of snow, blacked out, I let up on the gas, and in a split second the car stopped. So I started walking.

Next year I'll have snowshoes. I didn't think I'd need them, but in the north country you always need them, so starting now I'll save all pennies and by next year maybe I'll make it.

But I didn't have them that morning so I walked, hauling aching legs out of three-foot drifts, and stopping after each step to pull cap down, pull snow out of collar, shift tote bag with copy, mailing lists, galley proof, address changes from Florida back to Michigan, and bundle orders, from one aching arm to the other. But the highway was near and there I soon hooked a ride and another Call came out – right on the nose.

Mar 30, 1960

The move to Roscommon saved Marguerite from many dreaded winter drives to the printer, but on this day the snow did her in. Still, there was work to be done, necessitating a walk for two miles through the snow.

Confusion

I went to the pond for a walk, to the pond where a little breeze had cleared it of pine needles, where pines were reflected, where the banks were greening up and the salt block was a sorry shadow as deer licked it to a wisp.

I went to the pond, little to be sure, but quiet, a contemplative spot guaranteed to ease muscles that can make a stomach feel as though it's heading for the top of a jack pine. Summers get rough; so much to do, so many things going on; how to decide on what to cover. Cover the Midwest Fish and Game meeting and the Commission meeting or miss them and cover little towns and what folks are doing.

Another edition of The Call came out as workmen poured concrete, pulled out old walls, added new ones, as a big new room was added to The Roscommon Herald-News where The Call is printed. A new press was coming in. A new addressing system was being installed. New steel files were unloaded. All was in confusion. The Call had grown. The Herald-News folks had decided to shoot the works; and so work on a big new addition made the regular day just a bit more hectic. Three weeks of bedlam and the quiet pool was a welcome place to relax. There one could go but only after taking care of cabin chores.

Jul 19, 1961

*Nearly eight years from **The North Woods Call** beginning, this column shows that running a one-woman newspaper took a toll. Her pond and the surrounding woods at the cabin gave her solace. "Pine Whispers" provided her written therapy and became a window to her thoughts.*

Marguerite demanded the best product of herself. Her loyal readership had grown; so much so, that her printer had to expand and install new technology. The Call became bigger than the Roscommon paper that printed it. Gahagan had moved from Douglas Lake to become more efficient and make things easier but producing the paper remained a challenge.

Appointments

Perhaps I should put a little emphasis on the appointments since The Roscommon – Herald News gets phone calls requesting information on how to contact the editor of The North Woods Call.

The editor cannot be contacted except by mail. I have no phone. I live on a trail in the deep woods, which is just what I want, since writing and getting out a weekly paper alone demands quiet and peace. The editor is not antisocial. Anyone who wants to see me should write and make an appointment. I am gone on my beat from 8 a.m. to 5 p.m. on many days of the week. Unless appointments are made in advance, I will not be available, since other time is budgeted right to the half-hour on paper work, and one may not make exceptions since there is no give in the tight schedule of printing a weekly paper.

This is not a case of being high hat, difficult or hard-to-get. It is simply a matter of operating a business to make a living and pay the bills. Still impossible is the luxury of visiting anytime with anybody.

Of course there is an exception. That exception includes those specially privileged neighbors the little birds, and when deadlines press, when writing gets hard, I can always walk outside, toss out some seeds and listen to the lovely song of a chickadee when blizzards blow.

Jan 30, 1963

Just over nine years after the start of The Call, this piece describes Marguerite's life in a nutshell. The newspaper and the animals around her cabin were her life. And notice, still no telephone!

Address Mess

I could help my friends but there was little I could do for the cabin. There the mist had curled for many a day and night. There hung the unpleasant odor of mildew. I had hauled off mattresses. Sat them on end. Strung blankets, mattress covers, quilts on the line when the sun came out and a brisk breeze blew; started a big fan circulating heavy air. I had scrubbed gray-green off a wicker wastebasket, and burned paper daily lest it accumulate and add to the mildew smell. It was, therefore, nice to meet an Ann Arbor sportsman who confided that his winter outdoor leather boots had turned green.

The greenish shade of despair had settled over me, too. Last month The Call took a big step necessitated by growth. It went to stencils for its addresses instead of type. Type had piled up into galley after galley at The Roscommon Herald-News where The Call prints. Stencils would make checking easier, each filed under the town and in alphabetical order. That's what I thought.

But came the day when all the stencils arrived. They had been cut by the nation's old-timer in stencil pioneering. Their name had become synonymous with stencils. But it soon appeared that the company had failed to proof read the stencils against my original list. Subscribers were dropped. Towns were so misspelled that the Post Office could not deliver papers and so at five cents each I was deluged with papers undelivered. Then I had to have a new stencil cut, and send a back issue that a subscriber had missed. Digits in street numbers were transposed. Subscribers were put in wrong towns. Some subscribers were getting two papers as a result of duplications. All was chaos. I was deluged with complaints. I was fit to be tied.

Con't next pg

Address Mess

con't from previous page

When I went out to feed my dear neighbors in the pond only a fish trained in left field could catch a particle of bread. My whistle was off key when I called the chickadees and purple finches. I was indeed fit to be tied.

This horrible mess continues. All I can ask is that if your name or address is wrong, but that by some miracle you are still getting the paper, to please let me know, and if you know someone who isn't getting their paper to please explain this mess and urge them to alert me at once.

I am not alone in my misery. The Roscommon Herald-News had 400 subscribers' stencils cut for delivery at Houghton Lake instead of Roscommon and it was nice to have someone to commiserate with during this trying time.

Sep 20, 1961

As Marguerite increased attention to conservation issues, circulation increased. This necessitated changes at the paper to make distribution more efficient. Every new convenience seemed to cause a headache for the publisher, at least in the short run.

Tip Your Hats

Tip your collective hats, dear readers, to those four unsung troopers who went into the Mio District, and to Mr. Childs and his top brass who picked the cream of the crop, maybe not as to years of service, or Civil Service rating, but as to dedication and native smartness. They came, they worked, and they sure did a job.

Considering the dragging of feet by county prosecutors in the north country, and the disinclination of justices to throw the book at violators, they didn't give up but kept plugging. Their effect cannot be measured in the numbers of arrests, convictions or fines. But boy, oh boy, their impact will be felt for a couple of years on the native violators, who have now developed an almost permanent tick: looking over their shoulders every time they even think of violating.

Go in a little town in Oscoda County and ask a native about the swoopdown and everyone clams up. All they know is "I heard a guy say-". Said one, "That guy that pleaded guilty never should have done that. No jury ever convicted for deer killing around here."

Dec 5, 1962

Marguerite detested poachers, considering them thieves. At the time, she felt that there was little enforcement of game laws. Justices of the Peace generally handled the cases and they often looked the other way when it involved a local person.

Time To Say Thanks

If you want to collect a little of the fast-vanishing old north country, head for a bar and listen to the current furor. One unknown should get an earful. If you are known don't waste your time. But it is a fascinating part of the warp and woof of the changing pattern, the old giving way to the new; a new awareness that a natural resource, such as the deer, has a value, and belongs to the State.

The State Troopers may well have done what Conservation Department people and organized sportsmen have failed to do over all these years. They threw the fear of God into some of the natives and for sure. And while some still talk about "poor old Joe with six kids to feed", there is a feeling that welfare shouldn't have to pay for all those drinks poor old Joe had while hanging around a local bistro to make a contact with meat-hunting down-below deer hunters who had failed to connect, or a black market restaurant that wanted to serve a venison menu.

Dec 5, 1962

In late 1962, State Troopers took down a poaching ring. That got everybody's attention, including Gahagan, who praised the action in these two pieces.

Nightlife

Such a busy place is The Call cabin.

It was a warm night and only the screen door was closed. It had to be closed or friends would be rousting one out of bed all night. As it was the old mantle clock struck two as a horrible clatter arose on the porch.

Three raccoon friends were playing catch with empty, pans – empty of gumdrops, courtesy of Wayne County Sheriff Andy Baird. They had demolished the contents of a large cardboard carton of meat scraps, courtesy of Minnie and Mike, of the burg's grocery, and were in a mood to play.

Earlier in the evening I had fed a particularly dear friend a piece of bread with marmalade, and he had held my hand at the proper angle with a paw, and when through, had carefully licked each of my fingers, not only to clean them of goo, but to express thanks for the scratches under an itchy chin.

Four rose breasted grosbeaks share a 20-foot ground-table strewn with cracked corn and wildbird seed with two Blue Jays, so in love that they feed one another belying their usual tough-character roles: a White-throated Sparrow – who spatters silver notes of beauty in payment, a brown Thrasher kicking dry leaves high and wide; two Towhees talking, companionable and bouncing with joie de vivre, and an assortment of Starlings, horrible to behold, bowing, gorging themselves and thinking of all the nice handouts.

May 22, 1957

Among Marguerite's closest friends were her Little People, the animals she fed and conversed with at her cabin.

Batty

The editor and publisher of the North Woods Call stood off and looked in frustrated horror at her Alter Ego wielding a large broom and making wild passes at the graceful shadow of a bat cutting the no longer peace and quiet of the cabin.

The editor and publisher moaned in horror. "You can't do that. You can't really mean to swat that poor little bat," she said, and her Alter Ego screamed back in a voice resembling a fishwife's that she not only could but would, and the broom cut a wide swath in the air only inches behind the graceful bat zooming from living room to kitchen, past closed bedroom door into back hall.

"But think. Please think of all I've written about bats being inoffensive little creatures doing their bit for mankind by eating beetles and insects," argued the editor and publisher, but her Alter Ego swung the broom, missed by a wide foot, and left a little trail of spattered drops of honest sweat pouring off her face like rain.

"Listen, keep that line for your readers," said the Alter Ego. "I'm sick and tired of reading about being kind to wildlife. I don't like bats. Now I'm not sleeping in a bedroom with a bat. Last year one of those things fanned me three whole nights, missing my face by inches and whanged the bedroom screen, and you and all your high falutin' ideas can go hang. I'm out to get this one."

Strategy was in the making. Lights flicked on and off. A door was propped open giving wide-open access to all the bugs in the' north country that wanted to come in the cabin but also giving a wide-open invitation to the bat to get-the-heck out.

Aug 7, 1957

We all struggle with our conscience at times but few of us have to rectify it with what we preached in print!

Strictly Illegal

This is, to be sure, a serious violation of the law, according to Mr. Treat, head of this region's Conservation Department law administration division. Mr. Treat has pointed out before to The North Woods Call editor that feeding wild animals to the point where they could be classified as pets is illegal.

But The North Woods Call editor is going right ahead having found that all wild animals in her bailiwick have enormous and epicurean appetites.

What her guests do in their spare time, that is time not spent eating, is their own business in the best tradition of American freedom, and therefore in a journalistic interpretation of freedom, a matter of personal right and no business of the Conservation Department, let alone of The North Woods Call.

If the editor is sucker enough to lay out a delectable smorgasbord who should call it illegal?

Jul 6, 1955

Marguerite spent money feeding the animals around her cabins — first in Johannesburg and later in Roscommon at what is now the Marguerite Gahagan Nature Preserve. And where did the she get the money? Some funding came from readers who added a little cash to their subscriptions or Christmas cards to feed the characters featured in her "Pine Whispers" writings.

Acorns

There were three great oaks, ancient trees, and under them was a carpet of acorns. A red squirrel chattered. A chipmunk scolded. A blue jay cried in dismay.

I was harvesting acorns. Acorns are here and there but not everywhere. They are spotty.

I needed acorns for the long white winter when neighbors come and the larder is low. I gathered, keeping the good, discarding those with holes, and that my presence was resented, bothered me none. The earth was covered with acorns, huge, big, fat, luscious acorns. I wished the black squirrels that ripped up my feeders could have been with me. But it was all of nine miles from home, and there, wildlife pantries must be well stocked.

Heavy clouds threatened and at last broke, and my hunt ended, but I managed to gather some, thanks to a message from Roscommon's Bill Taylor alerting me to a spot where acorns were plentiful. How time changes things. Once it was Bill Taylor who gave me news on criminal cases he brought into Recorder's Court as a Detroit police officer. His message on acorns was better than details on crime. Even as I acquired quirks in my back and Charlie horses in my legs rushing to gather acorns before the gray clouds let loose a cold rain, I enjoyed it more than covering the marble halls of justice back in 1953.

Twelve years ago, after a long 12 years of living with crime reporting without a break. Another 12 years end this month: 12 years of The Call without a day off. How time flies. How the world changes. But how wonderful the world of the north country is in comparison to the world a news reporter lived in Detroit.

Oct 6, 1965

Okay! How many of you collected acorns and stored them to feed the wildlife in your yard last winter? And Marguerite gives us insight about her move north from the city. The work was hard but she did not regret the change.

The Mail & The Pantry

I had come from the Post Office. I decided to read my mail while sitting on the porch steps, warmed by the wonderful November sun on a late Indian Summer gift-day. Butch Chickadee was curious as he always is, very inquisitive. He hung from a feeder almost over my head and gossiped.

"Any interesting mail?" he asked. He knew very well that over half of the mail is interesting, in fact, fascinating. "Anybody interested in us chickadees?"

He also knew that was a sure thing. He picked up a sunflower seed, went to the window feeder ledge and hammered loudly on the seed which was actually a show, for he was so busy watching me that he dropped the seed. He hurriedly dived after it, caught it just as it touched the pine needles underneath, and returned to the ledge and waited for me to admire his thrifty ways as well as his agility. I did. He was pleased.

A white breasted nuthatch hung upside down on a big white pine trunk and in guttural tones said, "Well, is anyone writing to us?"

I opened more mail. I said, "You know very well that almost all these letters are from folks interested in you."

"OK," said Butch. "What I mean really is, are any of them sending grocery money?"

I screamed and the nuthatch flew right up to a high branch and marched up and down staring through the green needles to see if I was really angry.

"Grocery money," I repeated. "You are the richest birds in the north country. Right here," I said, waving a check and a letter, "Is a subscription renewal and a great, big, fat one buck for your feed."

con't next pg

The Mail & The Pantry

con't from previous page

Butch made a fancy curve over my head, his call echoing throughout the woods. A shy brown creeper moved hurriedly up a tree trunk, up, not down, and listened in amazement. Mrs. Hairy Woodpecker left a swinging suet bag in a loud flutter of wing feathers and landed on a dead oak and screamed so all the woods could hear. Then she beat out a wild tattoo. By then everyone knew the pantry was still full.

And I knew I had better come through. I went back in the cabin, leaving the lovely warm golden sunshine, and hurriedly mixed up a fresh and tasty dish of peanut butter thick with bread crumbs, cracked corn, millet and peanut hearts. Little dishes were filled.

Dec 5, 1962

Marguerite "encouraged" readers, with columns like this, to contribute money to her wildlife feeding fund. Subscriptions often arrived with a few extra dollars to fund tea time at the cabin.

Facts

Has The North Woods Call become a myth? A tale destined to grow with each repeating? In six years it has acquired considerable ink in the press. So perhaps one should set the record right.

The editor is not spending five bucks a day to feed the wildlife. I haven't five bucks a day to spend. I don't have five bucks a day to spend on myself. The wildlife gets fed, well fed, thanks to you and you and you, and unless a deer herd moves in and winter is another wingding we should get by for considerably less than five bucks a day.

For two weeks earlier this month, migrating flocks of birds kept me humping. Now they have gone. Only a dozen Juncos and a few stray Song Sparrows are still visiting. The regulars, of course, will stay with me: the Chickadees, Nuthatches, Blue Jays and Hairy and Downy Woodpeckers, the Grouse if they can get through the season.

Raccoons come and go, clean up scraps, dine on peanuts and gumdrops, get a taste for something else and head for the swamp, then come back. The Call is better situated with the swamp to receive wildlife patronage, and as time goes on more visitors will probably show up. The Snow-shoe Hare sticks close to his big brush pile and the fox family hasn't made up its mind if it is wise to return yet.

The Chipmunks are the most active right now. Junior Hoover Chipmunk sneaked in the garage, found the peanut sack and made himself almost sick. Such frustration. No ground in which to

Con't next pg

Facts

Con't from previous page

bury his find. Carefully he shucked peanuts and deposited them neatly in the four corners of the garage until I arrived and opened the door so he could go back to his warmer and more cozy home in the ground.

The hospital box has had a few occupants, birds that knocked themselves out on windows, but all have recovered. The last one, Mrs. Hairy Woodpecker, made a remarkable recovery considering how limp she was, how her long pink, thread-like tongue hung out.

Oct 28, 1959

Rumors circulated that Marguerite spent a large amount feeding the animals near her Roscommon cabin. Though her "friends" ate well, she would not have needed $5 per day to accomplish this in 1959. Marguerite wanted her readers to know that their donations were wisely spent.

Timing

Time schedules are important. Little People fed by you here at The Call must be kept on time. But I was late. I was late by a half hour getting home, and as I hurried to the pond with whole corn, two mallards, greatly upset, quacked loudly and took off. I should have fed no later than 6 p.m. I was a half hour late.

Feeders are again active. Male rose-breasted grosbeaks and male purple finches were waiting on feeders. I put out sunflower seeds, yours, so they could make before-going-to-bed feedings to young still in nests. Waiting at the porch steps was a large gentleman raccoon who knows that he is not yet quite accepted in the family circle of mama and three young. He received his can of dog food and three slices of bread.

Horrors. I had run out of bread the evening before and had to substitute nuts. Yes, they had a cracking good time, but they missed bread despite two full one pound coffee cans of Gravy Train. They spent the night going round and round the cabin, squabbling, growling, screeching, and the young bickering as they were trained. They did a masterful job in digging grubs. How thankful I am that I have no green, sodded, neatly mowed yard, just wild land, for there were dozens of neatly dug round holes, sand surrounding them as they dug for grubs.

Jul 17, 1968

The animals knew the schedule for the daily tea time, as Gahagan called it.

The Mob

There was the strange sound that makes one leap up and look. A stranger? Yes, and he slipped quickly into the woods, but talked. He was joined with two pals. They were scouts and they talked quietly and I listened.

The next day they returned. They moved among the huge pines, soared down to the pool, their talk growing louder with the squeaking cadence of rusty hinges. I shuddered. They had arrived.

They next day I heard them come, with quiet talk, and then they gave the signal and the mob moved in, almost a hundred grackles, and I moved out, cowbell in hand and clanged and what a mess it was, grackles squeaking and squawking, bell ringing, little birds chirping, Mama Bullhead fanning like mad over her pond nest, and all was confusion.

I walked the pond, cowbell clanging. The top boss grackle tested me. He waited, then when I'd moved 30 feet along the shore, he sneaked in, and I saw him and screamed and rang the bell and he went with rusty-hinge cussing and there was the loud rush of wings as the flock, covering swamp maples and black ash, cussed him out for having drawn them to a place where they'd be harassed. And temporary peace descended and a rose-breasted grosbeak male sang as he prepared to bring a young to a window feeder.

July 31, 1968

The cowbell – given to her by neighbors when she moved to Johannesburg in 1953 – remained an item of use 15 years later. Marguerite loved the wild animals in general but there were certain species for which she had no use!

The Pond

The pond has some residents. Seven bluegills are now cutting the surface, catching bugs, investigating their new home.

The pond, while still in the making, was a great source of curiosity to my neighbors. While the big shovel sat there overnight an inquisitive deer moved in to look things over. And as soon as water rose deer moved in, slipping on the still loose sand as they went to drink.

Long, long ago the land west of Roscommon Village was a giant beaver pond, and after it went out and settlers moved in, old beaver dams were found again and again. In front of my cabin is a swamp, the contour of a little creek that picks up speed a distance away as it heads north. But in front only its bed remained, wet pools in spring, good mosquito grounds, filled with brush.

Then came the great decision after a pinpointed check of the pennies. Make it a pond. Surely, with all those wet spots and the old creek bed, there would be springs, of course. And so I had the Steele boys come out, John, George, Jim and Jake, and they looked the situation over and studied things, and decided the pond should be a figure eight to save big handsome white and Norway pines, as well as a precious cedar. They decided to go in from the north rather than the south to save wild raisin and balsams, and they wheeled out their big stuff from town and dug the pond.

With each bite of the shovel we'd wait for a spring. On the west side

Con't next pg

The pond became the centerpiece of her new world at the cabin. Marguerite understood that the water would draw wildlife close to her picture window. Today, school children dip for aquatic insects in the pond, learning about nature's wonders as part of the Gahagan Nature Preserve's environmental education programs.

The Pond

Con't from previous page

the shovel chewed into clay. Surely here was a spring. No spring. One morning a nice bubble of water broke the surface of the south end, but it eased off and vanished. And the pond was done, just in the nick of time because deer season was ready to open and the Steele brothers wanted to go deer hunting. Then came rain and the pond was full of water that soon froze and not until spring did I know if I'd have a big empty hole or a pond. The pond had its water. Frogs moved in, a swelling chorus of nightly singers, and now a gift of fish. A wet spot on the west bank in the clay suggests that a spring is nearby. In the driest spring folks have known around here in a long time the pond has water.

Jun 7, 1961

Not Goodbye

How wonderful it is to know that I can write Pine Whispers without the deadline whiplash, always having to cut it off because of more important writing, getting ads, doing bookkeeping, sweating out make-up of pages, writing heads, watching correspondence pile up. So much to tell of spring as it comes and so little time to tell it. So many important matters in conservation of natural resources. And at long last there will be time to dig, write, inform you. For I am not going into hibernation. I will simply be released from small details that have overcome me as the paper grew bigger, bigger and was like holding a bear by the tail. The little paper, started November 11, 1953, with a blank page, is now the biggest circulation-wide weekly north of Bay City. How many more than the 9,000-plus known readers get it, as it is passed from hand to hand, no one knows.

Feb 26, 1969

The Call sold and Marguerite intended to continue doing what she always had – write. But just write. The demands of a one-person newspaper took its toll. She wrote the "Pine Whispers" column for the new owner for a short period then moved the column to the Bay City Times until 1982. Newspapers were her life for over 50 years.

Poetry From the Pines

There is a moment, a still short space of
time ... when time itself stands still.

And that still moment looms large in a
life.

It is but a moment in a lifetime,

A second of time to hold forever,

The slow movement of the ticking clock,

Marking forever something to hold and
never lose.

Time Is A Moment - 4/4/1956

"Poetry in the Pines" contains some of Marguerite's creative musings. Attuned to her natural surroundings, she described the environment quite elegantly in her *"Pine Whispers"* column. "Whispers" served as a vehicle for many of her thoughts and opinions, as well as stories of her Little People and her day-to-day life. Poetic descriptions of nature were often interwoven with these longer narratives. She sought out and savored the "moments" that make life in the north country so rich and rewarding. We have taken some liberties in this section; lifting some of her expressive sentences and paragraphs from these stories, editing them for length and reformatting them into verse. Though distilled, the essence of the writing remains and Marguerite's flair for the descriptive showcased. *North Woods Call* readers, who enjoyed her poetic meanderings, often asked Marguerite to publish her *"Pine Whispers"* in book form. She wistfully replied that the opportunity had never presented itself; that she did not know any publishers. We hope that our efforts would please both Marguerite and her subscribers. We also hope that today's readers can share in Marguerite's joy and appreciation of nature through her "poems."

The Maestro

Tall is the pine; the maestro conducting the woods symphony

Nostalgic memory of lovely moments

Heard throughout the woods by those who would but listen ... and try to understand.

The Maestro - 9/29/1954

Summer Samplings

Dragonflies, blue, green, iridescent,

Sail through gold sunlight,

Hover over heavy-headed grasses along the bank,

Skim low over green water,

Iridescent in the gold sunlight,

Little rainbows.

On The Stream - 8/3/1955

An insect rasps its song in the hot yellow sun.

In the breeze, gold leaves among the green of the birch
tell softly their message of red and gold to come.

The rich heavy gold of afternoon gives way to clouds of
wavering pale yellow,

As the sun comes over the hill, over the pines.

The blue heron walks in a world of golds ...

Gold lake lapping his legs, gold mist crowning his dark
crested head, gold scarf swathing his long, long
neck.

All Gold - 8/13/1958

The pond was clear ...

Clear of the golden dust of budding pines,

And the bullheads surfaced ...

During a brief, rainless period.

Life's Ways - 7/3/1968

*Inches from the lapping water's edge are the littlest of
the fishes.*

*So little they could not be seen except for their darting
numbers,*

Hundreds, almost transparent silver,

They play together in the shallow water,

Astonished at their new world.

Little Fishes - 7/31/1957

*Yellow buttercups, small, golden, shiny as though wet
with dew,*

Sway on slender stems on dry road sides,

Lifting their own sunshine above gravel patches.

The lovely cardinal flower, delicate orange-red,

Blooms in the deep woods, along damp trails,

*And a jack-in-the-pulpit is preaching for the wildflower
garden near the cabin.*

Glowing Colors - 6/8/1955

Wings a blur,

He hovered, darted, sped among the flowers,

Tiny body iridescent green, among red blooms.

Carefully he tipped his sword-like bill into each flower's
heart,

Methodically making the rounds.

Stopping a split second,

Remembered he had already emptied that one of its
sweetness,

Then, onto the next.

The sound of whirring wings, a tiny roar ...

Hummingbird dining.

Whirring Wings - 7/31/1957

The red wing blackbirds call from the willows ...

From a clump of reeds ...

A bull frog added his basso voice ...

The stream trilled over rocks ...

Mirrored in the water... stood the red-gold doe splashing water, music adding to the rhythm of the day ending ...

The frog and the stream sang on as the moon climbed the sky and the woods slept gently.

The Stream - 7/9/1958

Spitting clams resting peacefully on the golden sand

Become worried and close their shells,

And dig down in the sand.

Raccoons will find them ...

Digging with sensitive, knowing black fingers,

Not even watching what they are doing.

The lake's edge is laced with their paw prints;

All along here one hunted.

To open a shell tight-closed,

Is a secret raccoons do not divulge.

They turn their backs so you may not see

Just what magic they use ...

To unlock the shell pocketbook.

Lake's Lace - 7/31/1957

Dawn stepped through the north country coolly,

Trailing gray clouds of mist, she stepped from swale to lake.

Dawn swirled her gray chiffon,

Swirled in the little breeze that came with another shower,

Swirled her clouds of gray skirt,

And the east shore was here and then gone again.

White gulls screamed and cut across;

White appliqué on the swirling gray skirt of dawn.

Silver Rain - 7/27/1955

Golden days are arriving.

Overnight the black-eyed Susans appeared along roadsides,

Whole patches of them,

Taking over where daisies fade.

Golden Days - 7/15/1959

The fragile beauty of the spring flowers is but a
   memory.

Present now are the wildflowers of summer,

Wild daisies of white and gold,

Devil's paintbrush; orange-red splashes.

Blue vetch is in bloom, trailing tendrils;

A weed, but with its own beauty.

The spicy perfume of the wild rose, the swamp rose,

Five petals, simplicity ...

Sweetness on a hot day.

Bustin' Out - 6/29/1966

Bluebird,

Blueberries,

Morning sky, blue.

Along the road's edge ...

Blue notes in golden sunlight.

Blue Note - 7/31/1957

Far out on the lake a loon cried,

Seeking its mate

Lost in the pearl-gray swirling cloud of mist.

The cry pierced the swirling silver,

Echoing.

The cry was loneliness,

Agelessness, epitome of the primitive,

The last frontier between raw nature and civilization.

His black and white was lost.

His cry was silver splintering against silver.

Around the lake,

Around the world,

His cry could be heard.

Sound - 8/25/1954

There – in the opening in the pines –

Earth, warm with the sweet perfume of summer,

Berries ...

Black, blue, and many still green,

Delicious,

Sun-warm.

Soft plop of berry in pan,

Squeak of pail handle,

Dry blade of grass whispering as an insect leaps.

Stillness, quiet ...

Berry time.

Berry Time - 7/15/1959

Down on the beach sandpiper babies

Teeter on matchstick legs;

Small balls of gray and white

Trying to keep up to their peeping mother.

Children's Hour - 7/17/1954

Blue heron stands knee-deep in the lake.

He stands silently,

A gray-blue statue in the dawn's coming ...

Then moves stiff-legged through the bulrushes,

Seeking.

He lifts his crested head,

Stretches his magical, long neck;

Poised is he ...

And strikes.

Breakfast - 9/4/1957

113

He was butter-yellow;

Only a streak of black on the folded wings.

He was a secret moment,

A once-in-a-lifetime second,

Undiluted beauty.

He came down with speed,

Slackening to milkweed-lightness as he rested on the Sweet William in the yard.

The tall stem swayed only lightly, so daintily did he rest on the pink blossom.

The sun hit him ...

And he sat in a business-like manner as he sought seeds in the shocking pink.

Goldfinch, said the book,

Wild canary, said the mind;

Breathless beauty, said the heart.

Beauty - 7/7/1954

Across the sky, above the still blue water,

The bluebird dipped,

Sailed ...

Wings blue as the sky,

Blue as the water,

Turning for the sun to paint underbody pale gold and
pink.

And above him the eagle sailed,

No wing beat breaking the glide,

Nothing but silent rhythm,

Riding high, higher, higher,

Lost in the sky's blue, the sun's gold ...

Above the world touched by bluebird's wings.

Flying – 6/12/1957

Fireflies dance through the popple;

Small lights, small moons,

Blinking along the lake's edge.

Quiet Night - 6/19/1957

115

The sky darkened in the west.

A breeze swept through the trees, turning leaves over,

Showing their silver undersides.

Clouds moved northward,

The blue lake turned silver, the rain came.

Silver drops ringing the lake into a million circles,

Slipping in silver balls off the silver leaves.

The charcoal sky in the north blazed with lightning,

A mutter of thunder rolled and cracked.

The silver drops paused,

Then stopped ...

As a robin sang

And sandpipers raced low over the water's edge.

Silver World - 6/18/1958

Indianpipes gleam white

Moonlight pale ...

Silver ghosts in the dank forest.

Jeweled Carpet - 5/25/1955

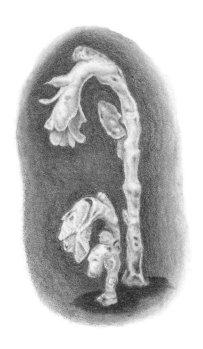

The Big Dipper

Moved,

Tilted,

Emptied.

The Milky Way spread across the sky.

The Spill - 8/25/1954

August is draping its gold and purple mantle over the
    north country.
Fields, plains, roadsides are lined with gold.
The gold of goldenrod ... small gold clusters weigh
    heavy the stems,
Weighed still more by drunken gold and black bees.
Gold in the north woods is the gold of pirates, of secret
    nuggets.
Each tiny blossom spills its gold along the branch;
Massing into moving, flowing waves of gold.

The purple is draped more slowly.
It is there in the blazing star, rising on stiff stems,
The royal crowns of the thistles.
Asters uncurling their own blue-purple, with flame-yellow
    hearts.

The countryside is purple, yellow, regal ... lace-edged;
Starched, white Queen Ann's Lace, secret delight of the
    eye and heart,
Edges the gold-purple mantle.
The mantle is royal, all glory, all beauty.
The woods wear it
With calm acceptance, with gentle dignity;
Theirs for the ages ... a natural heritage.

Royal Colors - 8/18/1954

Golden rays slide down the silken web

From bending branch

To sweet fern leaf ...

Turn dew drops into gold orbs,

Blaze diamonds of gold across red and green moss.

All Gold - 8/13/1958

The music ... seemed to echo.

One never knew from whence it came,

From which side, from the hills or from the swale,

But it came ...

Echoing music ... repeated call of the whippoorwill.

Whippoorwill - 6/12/1954

Gently the sun rose scattering starlight,

Breaking it into splinters.

Water lilies opened;

Over the swale, an eagle flew high

And a muskrat cut through the water to its home.

The rising sun was warm

And a young white-throated sparrow sang,

In off-key fragments,

Its lovely song.

It sang over cardinal flower red,

And water lily holding starlight and moonlight within.

Fall comes with ageless rhythm.

So Fragile - 8/24/1966

Autumn has arrived ...

Bracken turning yellow and brown;

A young maple boasting the first scarlet dress of the season;

Popple tossing golden leaves;

Tall, graceful, turkey-foot grass swaying along dusty roads.

In the fall sunshine,

The smell of wood smoke is incense on cold morning air.

September Song - 9/15/1954

Morning mist is heavy.

It hangs over the lake,

Until the autumn sun breaks through

To drive it off with the last of summer's heat.

And through the mist, down on the dock,

Stands an angular gray statue ...

Now hidden,

Now seen.

The blue heron fishes early these mornings.

Early Fishermen: - 9/15/1954

The sky was blue, the breeze soft,

Soft, as it sang goodbye to summer.

In the pond's mirror, pines stood tall and green;

Maple, flame-red; birch, gold.

Indian summer came to the woods,

And the little fishes rose until their fins cut the water.

Perhaps they too, sang,

"Mine eyes have seen the glory ..."

Color - 10/18/1961

Gold and black wings, so fragile,

Trembled in the warmth of the sun.

Some secret message to migrate;

Instinct of thousands of years.

The monarch butterflies

Resumed their thousand-mile trek.

So Fragile - 8/24/1966

Over the hills hangs a haze,

And the blue of the sky is a paler blue,

Paler, as is the sunshine.

September Song - 9/21/60

A sapling maple blazes red, scarlet, crimson;

A secret footstep in the north woods.

Blazing on the edge of the swamp, red, red leaves give
away the secret:

Autumn with her colorful skirts has stepped daintily
there.

Autumn flirts in secret, touching a maple here and
there.

The cold moon rides low in the sky.

Autumn Comes – 9/4/1957

Winter's knife, keen-edged,

Honed itself on the September white moon rays.

A moth, heavy-winged, cold;

A life nearly lived,

Flutters into the white moon's rays

And a nighthawk, hungry,

Cuts the still night to dine.

Winter's Knife - 9/26/1956

A storm in the woods is unlike a storm in the city.

In the woods the world is the cabin – four log walls –

Keeping out the rushing wind, the rain.

The power goes off.

The old kerosene lamp throws beams on golden walls.

There are nostalgic memories that belong

To the odor of the kerosene lamp,

The yellow flame held steady within the tall chimney.

Flames in the fireplace glow gold and blue.

A wet log hisses and crackles:

Small sounds as the thunder roars and chases,

Small flame as the lightning blazes across the sky.

It is still – even with the thunder, the beating rain.

Stillness of the woods alone, storm-tossed trees

And cabin of logs.

The Lamp - 9/10/1958

The orioles' nest is deserted;

All summer it hung on a popple branch not a third of an
   inch thick.

There it hung, swinging in the wind;

Rock-a-bye-baby for the small feathered ones within.

Six inches long and knitted together with a knit-one-purl-
   one stitch,

Soft grasses woven in and out of the pouch-like nest ...

Strong,

Graceful.

On the edge of the swale ... a hornets' nest,

Paper light, almost a foot high and ten inches wide;

Gray, egg-shaped masterpiece hung on a branch,

It withstood rain, sleet, snow, wind and sun ...

Paper-thin,

Invulnerable.

Out in the swale … muskrat houses

Tall mounds of branches, reeds, mud,

Delicately constructed …

Warm and dry in the harsh north winter.

Architecture that has served them for a thousand years.

Homes - 9/22/54

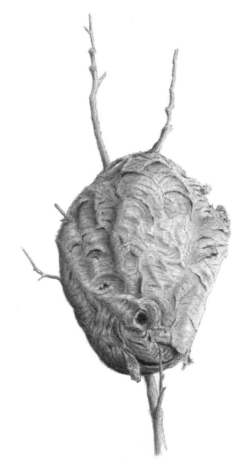

The sun catches the shades of green moss

Holding a tree's trunk warm against the earth,

Touches willow stems turning them jewel-red,

Slides its warm fingers down the old deer trail.

In the swamp the cold lingers,

But the rising sun finds the fragrant Cedar.

The rising sun touches the wild Mountain Ash,

Still treasuring orange-red berries;

Bright color rising above Cedar green.

The sun searches the swamp ...

Bringing all back to awakening day.

Awaking - 11/5/1958

The maple bends to see its scarlet self in the mist of the
    lake.

Autumn Night - 9/25/1957

It was twilight on the north branch of the AuSable:

It was the hour when woodcocks bathe in the sand of back woods trails. They huddled in the gray-brown sand, whirring their wings until the sand ran through their feathers, over their splotched backs, tossing their heads, delicate long bills cutting the twilight, beady round eyes watching the evening star through the small cloud of dust they happily raised.

Deer headed for the river to drink.

On a gentle rise, treeless, a curving line of the horizon, a deer stood silhouetted against the darkening sky. She tossed her head, she said something, and from the twilight lying on the rise below her was movement.

The little rise was broken. One silhouette was multiplied. Two fawns stood beside her. They turned to look at the nearby sound and then they were gone; over the rise of the hill, into the twilight descending over the AuSable.

Twilight - 9/1/1954

Rose-breasted grosbeaks prepare to go south.

Adult males have already gone;

Young birds will make the trip to Equador

Guided by the wise old females.

There will be a frost,

The stars will shine more brilliantly,

Soon will come a morning when my rose-breasted grosbeaks

Will not come for seed.

Mothers will lead the young on the long, long journey.

Godspeed, my friends,

Godspeed.

Godspeed - 9/21/1966

The Harvest Moon rose red, orange and gold over the
north woods;

The moon's silver flooded the woods.

Ducks cut a pattern, black wings beating the silver;

Arrows racing the moon.

Owls cried their high, wavering, achingly lonely
message.

Leaves drifted in the night's air,

Lisping silver whispers as they danced over resting
leaves.

Fall has come with quiet steps.

The Harvest Moon - 10/12/1955

The woodpecker beats a thunderous tattoo,

A salute to the wavering banner of fall,

Unfurled across the woods.

Autumn's Treasures - 10/16/1957

Near the beach in a little hollow was a half circle of white;

Mushrooms big and little.

Trailing up the bank were wild strawberries, leaves flaming red.

A cricket sang a brave, lonely song and back in the woods a woodcock called.

All around ... was the music of autumn,

Changing tempo ...

Fugue never played ...

Music felt ...

Never written.

So Quickly - 10/15/1958

Bright jewels of beauty,

Fall rains and sun brought them out.

Marching through the woods ...

Gold, ruby-red, blazing orange, pearl gray, doeskin
brown;

Little mushrooms ...

Toadstools of fall; all colors, all sizes.

One is seven inches across; its flat hat, butter-yellow.

A few feet away are two rubies no larger than a baby's
fingernail.

Orange ones grow near purple ones.

Some have caps of Chinese porcelain gray.

And then there are the beige, doe-shaded ones that look
old and weary;

Workers too tired to play with gold and ruby-red.

Throughout the woods they march.

They are here ...

It is their time of year.

Bright Jewels - 9/29/1954

Sumac lifts red spikes over angling rail fences climbing
the hill.

Ancient apple trees, where once jacks drove the big
wheels,

Scatter leaves to show red and yellow fruit

And under their burdened branches the dry grass is
bent.

There the doe, the buck, the shy fawns come to eat ...

Autumn treasure.

Autumn's Treasures - 10/16/1957

Leaves cover the woods floor,

Swish as one walks through them,

Smell of the richness of fall;

Scent lovelier than the perfumes of Araby.

Leaves, red, gold, brown, flutter silently as soft wings,

Warm, fragrant world ... fall.

Perfumes Of Araby - 10/5/1955

White mist swirled and parted,

Then the curtain dropped again

Over the AuSable at Twin Bridges.

And the little islands, green, diamond-studded

Were there and then gone,

Mysterious ...

Fairy-like.

Blazing Diamonds - 9/21/1955

Wet logs hissed and sang ...

Old pine knots smoked with fragrance.

Flames danced ...

Shadows on walls and ceiling

In ever changing pattern.

Mad music ...

In counterpoint to the rain.

Silver Fingers - 09/18/68

Against the black, they are suspended …

Like the eyes of witches.

Green sparks against the black velvet of night,

They hang in the air over bracken,

Under pine, under popple and birch.

They move, vanish,

Then are there again … green and round.

They blink …

Not fearsome,

Not witches,

But red-brown deer.

Questioning, inquisitive eyes stare into the brightness,

As man stares back, fascinated, questioning;

Wondering at the animal instinct of fear,

The animal art of camouflage,

The art of silence …

Part of the night's magic.

Witches' Eyes - 7/21/1954

Halloween;

Time of jack-o'-lanterns, trick or treat,

Playful masks and witches,

Arrived early in the north woods.

The Hunter's Moon, full red-orange moon,

Slipped over the pine ...

Pulled a lacy cloud over his face,

A secret mask,

And stared down at the quiet lake.

From the swale came the witches,

Hiding in gray mist, they danced over the lake.

A cricket struck up his fiddle and played,

A shorebird, migrating south, stopped to watch

And sing his lonely cry ...

Trick Or Treat - 10/21/1956

An acorn falls …

A hazelnut breaks its husk …

Busy tail flicks on a tree branch.

Gather, hunt, store.

Color must fade …

Color must go as jewel-leaves flutter

In their Autumn dance,

Flutter and fall, a sweet-scented woods carpet,

Leaving bare branches soon to be gentled with winter's
snows.

Some Will Go - 10/16/1957

The newly full moon grows cold,

Tells the wild wings they must move.

High in the sky the flights are on

And in the light of day there they are —

The great V wavering like gray smoke across the sky.

Muted Music - 11/4/1956

A great full moon, came swiftly over the hill in the east,

A monstrous silver bowl … rolling to a white path in the
sky …

White that crept into the woods between the oaks, the
hazelbush, the Juneberry …

Growing whiter, bigger, filling sky and earth.

All night the great moon lighted the sleeping woods …

Lighted the passage of those who only walk at night as
they stared at the moon,

That spills secret beauty … on a still, still world.

Harvest Moon - 10/8/1958

A blue jay …

Vivid lightning,

Flashes in the frost white of morning.

Frosted Beauty - 11/5/1958

Milkweed pods scatter white thistledown,

Down of fragile silver starred with gold,

And the branches of the pine hold the magic bouquet of make-believe.

The chickadee sees it — swinging like a tiny Christmas toy,

Sees it and flies to it;

Only to watch it float away on the wind from his wings.

Symphony In White - 11/5/1958

The hunter stalked, breath white in the wood's cold air,

Heart beating faster, faster at the sound of a leaf dropping,

Life becoming sweeter, dearer

As he walked alone in the woods.

Hunter's Red - 11/21/1956

The beauty of autumn fades, circle eternal, beauty not to be held.

An oak leaf in the world of brown, flamed, red it flamed in the afternoon sun.

Leaf of yesterday, part of the swing of the world

Faded leaf falling to earth, sun robbed, flame dim, sheltering the arbutus.

Faded leaf to know sunlight and spring and color again

On the next ...

Swinging circle.

Dim Flame - 10/29/1958

Winter Wonderland Words

In the old cutting, snowshoe rabbits play in the new world of winter, nibbling willow red and cedar green.

Empty milkweed pods are hinged with diamond flakes, stumps are white cushions plumped down along the road, oak leaves make whispered music with the wind and the snow and there is a new hushed quiet in the wood.

Snow buntings flock to roadsides, play in the wind-driven clouds of snow, and Blue Jays are at their bluest cutting through their world of white.

The miracle of winter comes with the brush strokes of snow white world, of muted blue shadows at dusk, of sparkling diamonds at dawn, of magic mystery with moonlight.

Holiday World - 12/3/1958

There is music in the air.

The east wind plays a symphony with the lake, wind lashing the little lake to chords that sing high, counterpoint to the wind singing in the pines ... and the wind in the oaks makes up the percussion section of the great symphony, singing the music of the sky, of the earth, of the world.

Rain beats on the roof, a thousand fingers playing against the roof, and the crescendo grows as rain turns to hail, white particles of ice hitting the cabin ...

The fireplace flares as wind, the east wind, swoops down the stone chimney, and logs spit and hiss and crack with the talkativeness of gossipy women ...

The fireplace blazes with light ... within the warm, safe cabin secure from the east wind waving its baton over the lake, playing its awesome music as the rain and the hail and the snow blare their trumpets, their brasses, their woodwinds.

Music In the Air -11/23/1955

The woods has many moods …

Sweetly musical,

A chickadee sang … answered by another;

Small musicians on a vast stage of white,

Fragrant with the odor of snow on balsam and cedar …

The woods has many moods.

Many Moods -1/5/1966

The cold crept through the white woods

And the stars in the dark sky crackled,

Starlight splintering against great fingers of northern lights.

And the otter …

Stood up

And stared,

His fur on end …

As though it crackled with the mysterious talking of the sky.

His Story - 12/20/1961

It was early morning, ... and on a bare branch of one of the old trees they sat, the two of them, staring into the east.

And the rising sun touched their great white-crested heads ... they looked with unblinking eyes, sitting side-by-side in motionless dignity; part of the woods, the muted quiet of the winter world ...

The sun rising higher brought warmth and life to the woods and the younger eagle turned his head, shook himself, the bright morning glow touching his feathers, and he spread his wings, filling the sky as he sailed in a wide curve from the tall pine, flying just to feel the freedom of wings strong ...

The old eagle turned his head slowly and watched his young ride the wind current ... ride the wind and then float down, down to light on a giant pine's bough, free and young and strong.

Free And Strong - 12/30/1959

The storm came with wild gusts of wind …

Tall trees bent, swayed,

Fought the shrieking wind,

Wind catching up whips of snow to slash and crack over the woods.

The wild whip snapped …

Curled, coiled, like a white snake writhing, striking,

White whip lashing …

And the woods was filled with the anger,

The fury of the wind.

Crack of branch flying,

Aching cry of limbs scraping.

And slowly, inevitably, wind and snow took over the woods covering all …

Leaving only great rhythmic waves of white,

Stretching fingers of white to clutch and trap.

The storm came …

It conquered.

The Whip Cracks -1/28/1959

At night the white and black world is different.

From the cabin one feels the mysticism ...

Artistry of a Japanese print.

Through the paned windows ...

A feeling of space ... geometric;

Pine boughs in the vase with the silvered milkweed pods

Black against the white,

Framed by the small panes of the window.

Arms of the jackpine cradling the snow ...

Angular, black lines against white space ...

A black and white etching through paned glass.

White World - 2/16/1955

Snow is gentle on tree branches,

Cupped in last year's empty nests,

Held in tiny chalices of empty seed pods ...

Now gentle-white.

Your Cards March - 12/25/1957

The sun broke red ...

Fiery streamers cutting the grey.

Gold rays touched the hoarfrost ...

Spilled diamonds red and gold.

On the snow the trail of the fox ...

Dazzling ...

Each paw print sparkling, cupped white fire.

Dawn - 2/14/1962

The mist hung like a white curtain over the woods,

Moving in an early morning breeze,

Parting, scattering; layers of white, of pale blue,

Ragged veils floating over the plains,

Touching the hardwoods ... all silver with hoarfrost,

Branches flaked with sparkling gems.

Birch were carved silver ... icy beauty among big pines.

The sun rose, whipping apart the mist veil

And the woods flamed all white and gold and diamond-
studded.

A stand of hardwoods became a fairyland;

Each branch thick with glittering jewels.

As far as the eye could see the white woods gleamed

And as a breeze tore at the thin veil,

Great flakes of gold-touched jewels floated down

To the white carpet covering the earth.

Hoarfrost - 2/21/1962

Off the road near a brush-pile are rabbit tracks

And a stream, blue as the sky, cutting under snow-heavy
banks …

Soaring high is an eagle …

The whole wide sky his alone.

Spring Blue - 2/25/1959

In the valley, a spikehorn buck stands frozen,

Only eyes and nostrils moving;

Gray-brown against the white valley.

Frosted Beauty - 1/15/1958

The woods is dressed befitting the holiday season,

Gold, white and diamond encrusted in the blazing light of the sun.

Firs wear white lace ruffles on each bough.

The tiniest balsam and the great white pines wear ribbons of snow,

Snow that sparkles red and green as the red sun rises

And with its rising the trees blaze gold, reflecting the sun ...

Part of a fairyland world.

Holiday Garb - 2/25/1963

Snow Buntings chirp carols as they swoop like flurries of snow flakes over white roads and fields.

Christmas Cards -12/14/1955

The tall mirror, the old mirror ... in its ancient, carved, walnut frame ...

One said "Merry Christmas" to it because in it, against its three-quarter century silver, were those one wished a Merry Christmas ...

They were there ... shadows never lost in the silvered glass ...

Mirrored for always, always alive,

Their smiles, their gestures ... memory of good times.

They were there ... passing across its polished surface.

The silver mirror caught the reflection, the passing image, the happy memory.

In its silver were ... those who had smiled and laughed and tilted hats, gathered folds of long skirts, straightened ties in high collars and stomped off the snows of yesteryears ...

Ever to be held, to be kept in quicksilver brightness.

The Mirror - 12/22/1954

Balsam branches were ski slides for little birds.

The Thaw - 2/7/1968

153

The cold wind sobbed in the branches

And swept across the lake all ice covered.

The cold wind beat against the trees ...

The littlest of them bent,

But came back to stand erect again in green dignity.

Another year had added another ring to the small trunk;

New strength to fight the wind and the cold

And the white snow heaped against it.

Another year was ahead.

The lake, ageless ...

As old as the glaciers that had carved its hollow

From the cold, frozen earth so long ago ...

Awaited the New Year.

Another Year - 12/26/1956

The fox cut across the trail,

Then headed for the swamp where a small stream moved swiftly, black against snow, moon lighted.

The fox moved over fairy tracks of squirrels,

Stopped to check along a fallen tree, moved on,

And hunted

… hard on tracks of mice,

… mouse tunnels from one tree root to another,

… thin shadows of white and gray in the light of the moon.

A fox dug, dug deep searching for the mouse,

And then moved on,

Nothing to show for his hunt …

But newly dug snow.

The Hunters -1/18/61

The logs in the cabin cracked like miniature cannons

And the thermometer outside rested on 25 below.

Down And Down - 2/19/1958

They swooped down the hill, through the trees, out on the lake, the whirling dervishes, white ghosts dancing their mad ballet, with the wind, the roaring wind, making their music.

Around and around they whirled, white robes twisting, fluttering, waving as they flung themselves in high leaps, high, high in the air touching the tree branches, and then kneeling, making obeisance to the east wind, flattening themselves on the white earth only to rise again, whirling, flinging themselves high.

The wind roared. It roared from the east and its music brought the mad dance to another climax, dancers rising from the swale, swooping in a chorus out of the swale across the lake; and down from the woods came others, swirling their whiteness about them, joining in the lake ballet.

And the wind music softened, faded, and the dancers fell to the snow, snow meeting snow, white dervishes motionless, their robes part of the wind-sculptured whiteness of the woods, the lake.

Drapes fell in gentle folds of white near the pine, near the popple. Soft folds, new on the path, showed where they waited for their encore, waited for the wood winds to whisper and the roar of the east wind to call them to their wild dance again.

Whirling Dervishes - 3/16/1955

A wire fence was a bejeweled spider web

A bird's nest ... a glittering bauble on a tree's arm

Dried weed-heads above the snow;

Miniature jeweled stickpins,

Holding the dazzling royal mantle closely to the earth.

White Waiths - 2/15/1956

On the pine the owl blinks great yellow eyes

And stares at the white moon in the deep blue sky ...

Great round black iris nearly eclipsing

The yellow moons of his eyes,

As he stares at the silent world.

As It Was Made - 1/23/1957

It climbed slowly.

It was an old moon, gentle with age, mellow, a little tired
as it charted its ageless course between the stars
gleaming white, shining blue against the dark blue,
sparking the water below with pinpoints of silver.
The old moon pulled itself higher into the north
woods sky, away from the pines, away from the
pine smoke curling from cabin chimneys, climbing
to shine on the deer.

The old moon lost its gold and found silver. The last
quarter sailed higher turning the woods into white
and black. It touched a wood pile and made it an
etching. It spread its silver to a brush pile jutting
into the lake and the brush pile was a dry point
masterpiece alive.

The Old One - 11/24/1954

There is something about the January thaw that is
unmatched.

It brings a certain goldness to the sun,

A wondrous secret in the wind,

A never-again heard note in the song of a bird,

A once-a-year fragrance of cedar, balsam and swamp.

It is all of winter unloosed.

The Thaw - 2/7/1968

Close to the silver morning star,

Hanging like a bright jewel in the pearl gray sky,

Was the last thin slice of moon.

Morning Melody - 2/2/1955

The wind is an artist ...

The north wind carves sculptures ...

Stark, angular, lines

Etched with gentleness,

Daring in its oft-repeated, familiar pattern ...

The wind cuts the snow ...

It cuts drifts of giant size

And minute drifts that would delight a jeweler.

Across the plains it carves its giant sculpture ...

Unencumbered by studio walls.

The tender curve of movement is there,

Liquid, sweeping, fluid ...

Carved in white snow,

Flowing from the sleeping pussy willow on road's edge

Up, up to the tall pine.

The snow flows as the wind molds it at will.

It flows over a stump, soft, rounded, gentle,

Life's source, silent majesty,

Earth sweetly swelling for the pine seedling.

It takes a popple as a starting point

And from that small dot cuts boldly

Through the woods to the road ...

Piles white on white with blue shadows,

In bold slashes, in angular, geometric rhythm,

Rising to a high point, high, high,

Then dropping abruptly,

Leaving the viewer breathless ...

Eternal masterpieces of cold wind, white snow.

The Master Sculptor - 3/21/1956

Chickadees are the spirit of the north country,

Of sunlight sparkling on snow,

Of strength, courage ...

Winged pixies carrying spring in their lovely songs.

Polar Bears -1/7/1959

Throughout the woods as day comes is a new note,

Heart-tugging notes of the chickadee's spring song,

Echoed from beyond the swamp ...

From the plains ...

From the jack pines.

A woodpecker calls loudly and then drills ...

The nuthatch talks with a liquid note,

A new sweetness ...

The sun rises higher and higher and icicles drip

And in dripping grow longer,

Swirled like candy canes.

A tiny insect, wings transparent, flies over the snow.

March brings new sounds ...

New feelings ...

A promise of spring.

A Promise - 3/7/1962

In the swamp the deer moved, moved deeper, floundering, pushing, hoofs small snow shoes ...

They fought the snow heavy with Spring's promise, snow wet, and stood, they who had lived the star-spangled nights, the nights of frozen breath and empty belly ...

They stood, sides heaving, caught, prisoner of winter's final cut with the scythe, caught there in world all white, life stirring, instinct to live driving ... driving heart to push ahead, push white snow, wet-heavy chains of iron, death.

And the pale sun cut through clouds of gray sky with crows flying, unhurried, low over world of melting white, world of loosening bounds, world with spring over the hill.

The Battle - 3/11/1959

A Chickadee, eager to burst the icy bonds of winter,

Sang his Spring song, as winter frost drifted through the
    air,

Sang his music of Spring; alone but believing.

The AuSable slept, unmoving,

Drooping willows on its bank ice-bound,

Rosy in the red-gold sun's dawning light, its promise.

The north woods trembled, shivered, stirred ...

Spring was upon it ...

Deep under its thick cold blanket of star-specked snow.

Waking World - 3/7/1956

The Milky Way sparkles against deep blue velvet

Like a Tiffany tiara

And the woods stir,

As they with velvet paws walk.

Autumn Comes - 9/4/1957

A single crow flaps slowly over the plains,

Still world, all white,

Cold.

But the sun and stars have spoken softly ...

Winter wanes.

They Know - 3/2/1960

It has been a spring of promises broken ...

Warm days and the sound of ice breaking,

Freshets rushing.

Then ...

Cold winter vengeance, snow flurries ...

Growing things stop,

Wait for a secret sign to again quicken ...

The pulse of life.

Broken Promises - 5/8/1968

Dawn rises over east banks touched by spring

Even as west hills wear tattered cloaks of winter white,

Worn garment torn by lake edge,

By warming Earth at trees roots,

By hollows where deer slept.

Dawn comes to the world so long silent,

Comes now with music ...

Questioning notes of a single robin,

Song of a sparrow singing to the sky.

Pink Dawn - 4/15/1959

The sun climbs higher, warmer,

Silence gives way to bursts of song ...

Robins insist spring is here to stay.

Rustle Of Spring / Good Break - 4/15/1959

Winter ice has scooped the bottom of the lake ...

... twisted, silver-gray driftwood

... old logs from when they lumbered

... big stones and little stones

... shells, so many shells

... a rusty tin can

... an old bottle.

All thrown by the awakening lake on the beach,

As the ice melts and recedes.

The Beach - 4/10/1957

The swamp, snow choked,

Became a pool-filled stage where small musicians performed.

Spring peepers found hummocks of sere grass,

Islands in lakes of cold snow water,

And sang in a variety of keys.

All singing the same song in wondrous harmony ...

They sang of spring.

The Dance - 4/20/1960

The woods awakened.

The sky filled with sunlight and soft breezes and life,

Singing, wonderful life.

The lake danced and its waters rocked the loon.

The loon, black and white on blue, lifted his head,

Called his cry of freedom.

The sky echoed it.

And echoed the wild geese,

Strong wings beating in unison,

A giant V heading north, ever talking.

The rain came,

And the spring peepers sang,

Filling the world with songs.

Early Spring - 5/1/957

The stream, so long ice-bound, rushes high

Touching banks long dry.

Near the wing dam a fisherman,

Legs braced against the current,

Casts again and again.

Opens his creel to touch the fish,

Jeweled colors on silver,

Rhythmic curve of the stream in their length,

Glitter of moonlight on ice in their fins.

Burst of beauty,

Spring's glory.

Spring Ritual – 5/13/1959

A heart stopping loveliness …

The first spring call of the whippoorwill.

It comes distant but clear over woods and lake as twilight
falls.

The call, whip–poor–will, whip–poor–will,

Breaks the evening silence

With the same melody sung by the pale evening stars.

He's home again.

Night Artist - 5/18/1955

The hare moves like a mirage through the woods;

White on white, brown on brown,

Changing as his earth changes.

Ears alert, listening.

Faint song of frozen crystal melting,

Of weed leaf rising,

The ears of the hare catch the small songs of spring.

Rustle Of Spring - 4/15/1959

High above the forest floor the pines talk to the moon;

Wind-talk high in the sky

As below, new life in changeless pattern flows.

Popple leaf uncurling,

Small maple pushing upward,

Balsam seedling swelling in an old stump.

Moon and tall pines in the stillness of night,

Ageless,

Watching the cycle of life unfolding.

Night Talk - 5/27/1959

Spring came quietly in the mist and rain

Then stood ...

Lovely, in a moment of sunshine.

So Quietly - 5/18/1960

173

The dogwood of the north country is known as red osier.

One comes upon it in the swamps and along the streams,

Adding its spring color even in winter.

And come June, it will wave its small clusters of little white blossoms

Over woods creatures seeking its shade.

Red Osier - 3/23/1955

The fog came quietly,

Without movement, not twisting,

Not turning in wild dances as it sometimes comes;

But quietly, so quietly.

It thickened and smothered out the world,

Cutting off the lake so near into another world,

Leaving only a few trees around the cabin,

And it was still ...

So very still and gray.

The Fog - 3/16/1957

There is a lush, heavy scent in the swamp

As life is renewed.

Moss grows velvet-green on long-fallen logs,

Wild violets are blue as the sky.

A woodcock calls as it hunts in dark shadows.

A spring bubbles up under a cedar's root

And idles on a northward trail.

The earth rises,

Willows giving way to birch, to popple, to jacks.

Nearby is a caterpillar nest, a great white 'V.'

The caterpillars,

Defoliating ...

An enemy the lovely trees must live with.

In Bloom / In the Woods - 5/27/1964

175

A log, huge, raised from the ground by its massive
   trunk,

Thickly covered with moss…

Except one spot.

That spot is polished, smooth, worn free,

Showing the ancient passage of beetle and worm in
   delicate tracery.

It is there the ruffed grouse drums,

Hour after hour, wingtips wearing smooth the trunk.

The ruffed grouse surveys his world … sends his message
   winging.

A Song - 5/25/1960

The swamp comes close to the trail road.

It is lined with cedar; green, fragrant, lacy.

In the spring,

Yellow moccasin flowers needlepoint a pattern against
the green.

Swamp Treasures - 8/31/1955

Pussy willows are ...

Spring on a branch.

Planting The Seed - 4/3/1957

The same color as the brown leaves

Covering the damp earth,

They fade into the background, an inch from a
moccasined foot

... another bit of brown

... an upcurled leaf

... a bit of dead wood.

Once taught to see them there were dozens, hundreds;

Small brown pixies pushing brown leaves aside

To thrust their tender, crinkled hats into the sunlight.

The morels, mushrooms of the Michigan north woods,

Cover the forest floor, heavy with the deep forest odor
of dampness,

New life.

A fragrance all their own.

Brown Pixies – 4/28/1954

May has come.

May with her violets,

Green leaves against the brown of the woods floor.

May with her carpet of arbutus,

Already growing pink with spring's age.

May with her speckled adder's tongue;

Spring beauties,

Wild strawberry runners, green, green.

Morels push sodden leaves aside with infinitesimal
patience, massive strength,

To poke brown heads up toward the sun.

May has come.

May - 5/4/1955

It rained all week.

On some days it came in scattered showers, gray-black clouds breaking before an eye-blinding sun that burned the rain drops on leaves and branches into millions of hanging diamonds. As the sun came out and blue patches appeared, robins flew like red arrows to tree tops and sang their jubilation. Song sparrows shook wet brown fluff to look rounder and rounder, and sang loudly as though trying to drown out all competitors.

Another day the rain came with mist; curling, white and gray ghosts of mist sweeping over the lake from the swale, turning in torturous shapes at the fancy of the wind that played with the pearl-gray wisps. The gray lake would be beneath the ghosts, and then there would be no lake at all; only gray whirling shapes shutting off the horizon, bringing the end of nowhere closer and closer to one staring, trying to pierce the grayness to the beyond.

Again it rained and the drops turned the lake into a pattern of small circles. A sandpiper flew low near the shoreline riding the wind as he came in to land on thin, stiff legs, crying his troubles. Sun-baked bracken, wintergreen, and partridgeberry grew greener before one's eyes. Oaks began dropping long cherished brown leaves of last year, and fat buds grew plumper as the rains came.

The rain hit the cabin roof. Sometimes it was but a whisper, soft as gentle dew, water dripping from the eaves the only really tangible proof that there was rain. And then it came harder, harder, pounding its rhythmic beat, sweeping in gusts as the wind pushed it, as the trees bent and showered down their own leaf-filled drops.

Wet sand drifted into strange, geometric patterns along the paths and mornings bore clear, perfect imprints of woods visitors; bunnies, skunks, porkies, raccoons, deer. Even the delicate, faint marks of the chipmunk were held in the wet, rain-soaked sand, the diary of the woods. Outside it smells clean, washed, fresh. Green things seem eager to grow, to push their way up and out, to flaunt their beauty, their color, their fragrance.

The rain fell all week. And when it ended a new world welcomed the blue of the sky, the gold of the sun, the seeking eye, the breathless wonderment.

Rain - 6/9/1954

Small birds – fast climbing –

One with the wind

Curving ... circling ... rising ... diving

Joining the wild dance,

Then riding quietly ...

Alone.

Flying - 8/20/1958

The old trail is almost lost in new growth.

I must stand and find my bearings ...

Here is an aspen ... a tender sprout yesterday,

Now a strong sapling.

The Old Path - 9/4/1968

Jacks-in-the-pulpit ...

White violets ... deep purple violets ...

And some soft, sky-blue ones.

White trilliums fade to rose,

Pink ladyslippers wave small shoes in the breeze,

Juneberry bushes show small green berries,

And huckleberries are in bloom.

Pines shower gold clouds from yellow candle-blossoms,

Crushed leaf of newly green sweetfern is rare perfume.

Deep in the woods,

Gnarled branches of old apple trees

Shower white and pink blossoms ...

Where the doe lies

With her spotted fawn.

Jeweled Carpet - 6/5/1957

The lake was in a magical mood this morning.

The loon called his primitive, eerie call to a mate hidden in the gold cloud.

It was a secret dawn,

A dawn made for the long ago,

When the red man slipped through the gold cloud in his birch bark canoe;

Silent paddle dipping gold into gold.

A sandpiper came in low;

A golden ghost cutting through the mist, gone into the gold cloud,

His cry muffled in mystery.

The sun rose higher, and the lake slowly pushed its golden blanket aside.

Dawn ending ...

Day breaking.

Golden Lake - 7/17/1954

The lake moved like a thing alive as the wind hit,

It was all rhythm, all movement.

The rain came,

Silver fingers hitting silver.

The gray sky shifted, changed as the wind danced,

And the sun came.

A rainbow hid its pot of gold in the woods on the hill.

Pot Of Gold - 07/24/1957

Outside, the Norways and white pines bend gently over
the cabin;

Home ...

How dear it is.

How dear the woods around me,

Its quiet, its wonder, its life.

And they of the woods – neighbors – make me feel at
home.

Stories - 9/30/59

The Preserve

Opening up the swamp with the
pond offers a happy combination of
sunlight and dampness, an opportunity
to experiment, to transplant, to
consider seasons with their priceless
gifts, a chance to combine, balance,
manipulate, test, experiment. Pine
needles shedding this fall will build
humus, as will the leaves of the ash,
the birch, the popple and oaks that
are on the line of transition, for
in back of the cabin it is plains, a
land of oaks and maples, sweetfern and
blueberry, young white pine head high
seeded by the old giants in the front
yard, and plume-like young Norways.
Only the cedar stands alone; old,
browsed high, no new growth. Young
birch is finger-thick, and, willow is
a tangle along the old stream bed as
the flow picks up.

The North Woods Call - Aug 9, 1961

Fifty years ago, shortly after she moved to her new cabin, Marguerite Gahagan had a pond dug. She hoped that the excavation would hit a spring and produce a flow but had to settle for a seasonal, vernal pond instead. In her newspaper, she frequently wrote about life in and around this pool. Now the pond and the woods, along with her cabin, are prominent features of a nature preserve established by her estate. Marguerite wanted the area to remain natural so others could enjoy what she enjoyed.

Today, school children kneel on the pond's deck, scooping up pond organisms to later investigate under a magnifying glass or with a projecting microscope. A look at the variety

 of squirming, flailing aquatic life never fails to amaze! This is only a part of how Marguerite's woods and wetlands are used today. But how did we get here?

Creation of a Preserve

In the fall of 1994, Marguerite's health declined sharply. Needing extensive care, she was unable to live in her home for her remaining years. The vacant cabin was vandalized, prompting Marguerite's estate to begin executing her will.

Furnishings and other items were auctioned with proceeds donated to Kirtland Community College. The DNR received

her home and property with the stipulation that it be used as a nature preserve or sold at auction with the proceeds going to support conservation education. Thanks to some truly heroic efforts, the Roscommon Metropolitan Recreational Authority (RMRA) acquired a special use permit for the property from the DNR in 1996. An organizational meeting held in Marguerite's home a month later established the Marguerite Gahagan Nature Preserve. A substantial gift from Marguerite's estate in May 1998 allowed RMRA to purchase an additional 9 acres plus an easement that connects the Preserve with an adjacent neighborhood and nearby Roscommon schools. The legislature transferred another 40 acres from the DNR in December of 1998. The village of Roscommon provided one more acre as a green buffer zone with the adjacent industrial park. Following the appointment of the first board of directors in autumn of 1998, the Marguerite Gahagan Estate Trust transferred the balance of her assets to help operate the Preserve.

Marguerite's cabin, pond and woods serve as a classroom for environmental education programs conducted at minimal cost to area schools. In the summer, Gahagan Preserve puts on a three day camp. Preserve photos by Jeremy Jones.

Come Visit – Come Join Us

Need a break from your routine? Come visit Marguerite's woods. Her Little People still live here and invite you to stop by. Several miles of paths weave through the property and some are paved and wheelchair-friendly. Keep a sharp eye out and you may spot a raccoon, a deer or a chipmunk. Listen and you may hear the barred owl cry. Linger by the pond or search for the start of Tank Creek near the gazebo. Eye the huge pines, hemlock and cedars. Marguerite Gahagan gave you her home and its back woods.

The Gahagan Preserve is more than woods though. We provide environmental education, both on-site and off, to schools in a four-county area. Pond study is just one of a wide range of topics designed to enhance and complement each grade's science curriculum. Hundreds of school children benefit from special programs presented in their own classrooms or field trips to the preserve every year. Additionally, Gahagan hosts a nature day camp for children each July. Several times a year, we conduct nature presentations for people of all ages.

Our volunteers also founded and coordinate the Upper AuSable River Watershed Monitoring Program. Twice a year, citizens, including area angler and river groups, sample aquatic organisms from the river and its tributaries to keep tabs on the stream's health. Kirtland Community College lends us their laboratory to analyze the samples.

The Marguerite Gahagan Nature Preserve has grown in both size and scope over the years. It is a volunteer organization. Its accomplishments depend on people who love the outdoors, value the environment and realize the need to educate our youth about the natural world.

Find out more: **www.GahaganNature.org**

Marguerite Gahagan Nature Preserve

209 Maplehurst Rd. Roscommon, MI
at the end of Southline Rd.

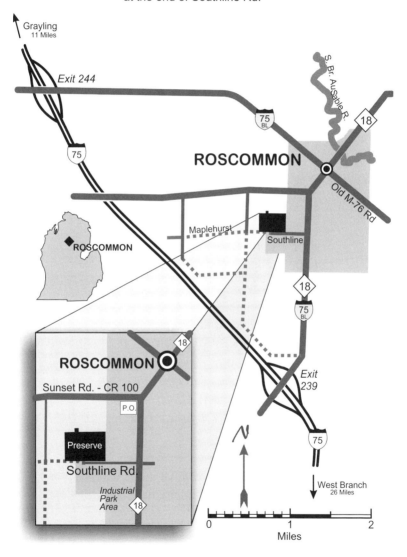

> Tomorrow's generations must know what the balance of nature means, and no textbook has been written, or laboratory conceived that can surpass a personal acquaintance with a pond and its life-cycle, woods and its development, or the personal bond that comes with the smell and feel and friendship of earth and its gifts of plants and wildlife.
>
> **- Marguerite Gahagan**

Marguerite Gahagan Nature Preserve protects wildlife habitat from development and educates about the value of wildlife and our natural world. Please consider helping with this legacy by

* *Becoming a member*
* *Making a donation*
* *Considering memorial giving*
* *Volunteering for cabin, grounds and trail maintenance*

Area teachers can
* *Request an environmental education field trip during September, October, May or June.*
* *Have the Gahagan Visiting Naturalist Program come to your classroom during February, March or April.*
* *Utilize Gahagan's ELF (Environmental Learning for the Future) study programs and kits.*

Trail maps, the Preserve's calendar, news updates plus information on purchasing additional copies of *Pine Whispers* can be found at our website.

www.GahaganNature.org